DESTINY AWAKENED
WHEN FAITH MEETS GOD'S MIRACLES

BY JOSHUA L NEAL

Dedication

I wholeheartedly dedicate this book to Pastor Greg Mitchell, my pastor and leader, whose life has been a pattern of someone who has seized destiny with faith and conviction. As his disciple, I have been blessed to learn from his example of unwavering commitment to God's calling. He has not only embraced his own destiny but has also guided and inspired countless disciples and leaders to step into theirs. His life is a testament to what it means to walk boldly in faith, and I am deeply grateful for his impact on my destiny in Christ.

Acknowledgment

I extend my heartfelt gratitude to my Spanish translators, Miguel Delgado, an evangelist, and Fabian Godano, a pastor. Your dedication and expertise have been invaluable in bringing my book to Spanish-speaking readers. Thank you for your time, effort, and commitment to this project—I truly appreciate your support.

About The Author

Joshua Neal is a devoted follower of Jesus Christ whose life was transformed through the power of salvation in Santa Fe. Born again and forever changed, he was saved at The Potter's House Church in Santa Fe, New Mexico and then later discipled at The Potter's House in Prescott, Arizona, under the leadership of Pastor Greg Mitchell.

Joshua's journey in ministry has been a dynamic and fulfilling adventure alongside his lovely wife, Melanie, and their three children. Together, they have faithfully pastored churches in Albuquerque, New Mexico; Huntsville and Athens, Alabama; Lawrenceville, Georgia; and for the past nine years, in Blythe, California. Under his leadership, their church has not only thrived locally but has also sent out churches to various parts of the world, expanding the reach of God's Kingdom.

In addition to his pastoral work, Joshua has a passion for writing. While he has authored children's books, Destiny Awakened: When Faith Meets God's Miracles marks his first Christian book for a broader audience. Through this work, Joshua hopes to inspire and encourage people to embrace God's plans for their lives, step boldly into their destinies, and trust in the miraculous power of faith.

Joshua Neal's heart for God, family, and ministry shines through every page, as he shares lessons learned from his walk with Christ and his commitment to advancing the Kingdom of God.

Table of Contents

Dedication ii

Acknowledgment iii

About The Author iv

Prologue 1

1. Destiny On The Shelf: Unleashing God's Purpose In A Life Left Waiting 4

2. Embarking On Destiny: Crossing The Threshold To God'S Promises 9

3. Embracing Destiny: When God's Plan Becomes Our Own 15

4. Obtaining Destiny: The Journey To God's Promise 20

5. Destiny In Babylon: Character Counts 27

6. Examined Destiny: Examining The Soul Of True Discipleship 38

7. Fruitful Destiny: Destined To Bear Fruit 50

8. Fulfilled Destiny: Moving Away From The Familiar 58

9. Destiny & Marriage: God's Plan For Unity And Purpose 65

10. Fulfilled Destiny: The Overall Picture 73

11. Crossroads Of Destiny: How God Shapes Hearts For His Purpose 80

12. Destiny Alliances: Strong And Wrong Alliances 87

13. Destiny In The Middle Of His Will: Finding Purpose Through Life's Troubles 93

14. Evangelistic Destiny: Empowered To Reach The World 99

15. Destiny Dominion: Re-Establishing Dominion 105

16. Guarding Destiny: Protecting the treasure within 111

17. Destined To Stand In The Gap: Answering God's Call 117

ALTAR CALL 123

Prologue

"Destiny is not a matter of chance but it is a matter of choice" -**Anon**

Destiny is often spoken of as though it were a distant horizon—something to be reached or uncovered only after years of searching, striving, and waiting. But what if destiny isn't as far away as we think? What if, in truth, it is awakening within us even now, waiting for the moment when faith collides with God's miraculous power?

Every person has a destiny—a divine blueprint designed by the Creator before the foundation of the world. The Bible assures us of this when it says:

> *"For we are His workmanship, created in Christ Jesus for good works, which God prepared beforehand that we should walk in them"* (Ephesians 2:10, NKJV).

Yet, too often, life's challenges, distractions, and disappointments leave us questioning whether this destiny will ever be realized.

But here's the truth: destiny is not merely about where we are going; it's about who we are becoming. It is shaped by the decisions we make when life gets hard, by the faith we cling to when miracles feel far away, and by the resolve to trust God even when the path ahead seems uncertain.

Throughout history, men and women of faith have encountered moments where their destiny awakened. For Abraham, it was a call to leave everything familiar and follow God into the unknown. For Joseph, it was standing firm in the midst of betrayal, slavery, and false accusations. For Esther, it was the courage to step forward and say, "If I perish, I perish." And for Daniel, it was purposing in his heart to remain faithful in the face of Babylon's temptations.

These moments of awakening were not the result of human effort alone. They were divine appointments—miraculous intersections of faith and God's power. In these moments, the ordinary became extraordinary, and lives were forever transformed.

What about you? Perhaps you feel stuck in a season of waiting, questioning whether God still has a plan for your life. Maybe you're facing circumstances that seem insurmountable, or you've allowed fear and doubt to overshadow your faith. Wherever you are, know this: your destiny is not lost. It is waiting for you to awaken to it.

This book is not just about miracles; it's about the God who performs them. It's about the faith that unlocks doors, the obedience that moves mountains, and the hope that refuses to be conquered. It's about discovering that when your faith meets God's miraculous power, nothing is impossible.

The journey ahead is one of revelation, transformation, and divine encounter. Are you ready to awaken to your destiny? If so, take a deep breath, open your heart, and prepare to see God move in ways you never imagined. Your destiny awaits, and the miracle-working God who designed it is ready to meet you on the path.

This is your moment. This is your awakening. Welcome to the journey.

By Joshua L Neal

1. Destiny On The Shelf:
Unleashing God's Purpose In A Life Left Waiting

Niccolò Paganini's violin sat in silence. It had once been the world's envy, producing beautiful music that audiences believed was touched by the divine. Yet there it lay, encased in glass, forbidden to sing again. Paganini's wish, his legacy to the city of Genoa, had one fatal condition: the violin must never be played.

What no one anticipated was the betrayal of time. Wooden violins, it turns out, don't survive inactivity. They thrive when handled, caressed by a musician's hands, and tested by the strains of melody. Paganini's once-pristine instrument succumbed to rot. Worm-eaten and useless, it became a relic—a shadow of its former glory.

That violin, crumbling behind glass, symbolizes lives left unused, gifts shelved, and destinies deferred.

David didn't know he was walking into history when his father, Jesse, sent him on what seemed like an ordinary errand.

"Take these ten loaves of bread and some cheese to your brothers," Jesse instructed.

David obeyed without protest, leaving his sheep with a keeper and making the journey to the Valley of Elah. When he arrived, the scene was chaos. Two armies stood in fierce opposition—Israelites and Philistines. The battlefield echoed with a sound that set David's blood boiling: the mocking voice of Goliath, a towering warrior who defied God's army with every word.

"Who does this uncircumcised Philistine think he is?" David asked, his voice cutting through the murmurs of fear. "How dare he defy the armies of the living God?"

Destiny has a strange way of sneaking up on us in the guise of routine. David's story reminds us that opportunities to fulfill our purpose are often presented as mundane tasks. It wasn't an angelic visitation or a grand revelation that propelled David toward his moment of greatness—it was delivering bread and cheese.

Too often, we wait for something extraordinary to validate our calling. We imagine destiny as a neon sign or a loudspeaker from heaven, but more often, it's hidden in the rhythm of everyday life.

Like Paganini's violin, the real tragedy lies in those who leave their destiny on the shelf. Fear, doubt, and discouragement act like the glass case, trapping potential behind excuses and "what-ifs."

As David surveyed the battlefield, it became clear that fear had paralyzed Israel's army. Once brave and battle-hardened, the soldiers trembled at the sight of Goliath.

"Have you seen this man?" they whispered among themselves.

But David didn't see what they saw. Where others saw an unbeatable giant, David saw an opportunity for God's glory.

Sometimes, the greatest obstacle to destiny isn't external—it's the voices around us.

David's brothers, particularly Eliab, were quick to discourage him.

"What are you doing here?" Eliab snapped. "Who's watching those few sheep in the wilderness? I know how conceited you are. You just want to watch the battle."

It's striking how often those closest to us become the loudest critics. Eliab's words were laced with jealousy and dismissal. He sought to remind David of his "place" to shrink him back into the confines of his past.

But David didn't let the negativity stop him. He understood a profound truth: God orchestrates destiny.

Ultimately fear will cause us to shelf our destiny.

The soldiers' dread of Goliath had rendered them ineffective, paralyzed by the enormity of the challenge. Fear whispered in their ears, advising them against stepping forward. "What if I fail? What if the giant kills me?" Fear has a way of causing us to imagine ourselves in utter defeat and failure.

But David's faith gave him a different perspective. He saw the giant not just as an obstacle but also a hindrance to God's plan. For David, the battle wasn't about personal glory but defending God's name and fulfilling a greater purpose.

"The Lord doesn't save with sword and spear," David later declared. "The battle is the Lord's."

How many of us have allowed fear to shelve our destiny? We listen to the voices of doubt:

- "You're not qualified."
- "You've never done this before."
- "What if you fail?"

These lies paralyze us, convincing us to keep our potential locked away like that violin. But just as Paganini's violin was meant to be played, our lives are meant to be lived—fully and boldly, in tune with God's purpose. David understood what we must and that is that God gets the glory. Charles Spurgeon once said "We will only glory in God when we have first stopped glorying in ourselves." For David there was no turning back when David stepped into the valley to face Goliath. He didn't carry an escape plan or a contingency. All he had was a slingshot, five smooth stones, and unwavering trust in God.

Destiny demands risk. It requires us to weigh the fear of failure against the joy of fulfilling God's plan. Like David, we must enter the arena, knowing that the battle is not ours alone. When David walked into the ravine, he had an all or nothing attitude. David was willing to risk it all. Our destiny must be jumped into with both feet.

For some of us, it's time to take our destinies off the shelf, dust off the excuses, deal with our fears and step into the calling God has prepared for us. What a tormenting thought to walk by our destiny on a shelf and wonder what could of been. As David's story shows, God doesn't require perfection or experience—just faith and obedience.

Your destiny isn't just about you; it's about the glory of the One who fights alongside you. The truth is you can start now!

So, pick up your slingshot. The world is waiting.

2. Embarking On Destiny:
Crossing The Threshold To God'S Promises

The Israelites crossing the Jordan River in Joshua 4 is more than just an account of a miraculous event; it's a testament to God's faithfulness and a challenge for us to step into the destiny He has prepared. It's about leaving behind a life of bondage and embracing a future of promise, ownership, and fulfillment. Yet, as we'll see, embarking on destiny is no easy feat—it requires faith, courage, and determination to move forward despite obstacles.

To understand the significance of the Israelites' crossing, we must reflect on who they were before God called them. For generations, they lived in Egypt, oppressed under the weight of slavery. Forced to make bricks without straw, their lives were a picture of what the enemy does to those in bondage: stripping them of dignity, purpose, and hope.

A slave mentality began to define them—where ownership was nonexistent, and hard work only tightened the chains of oppression. In many ways, this mirrors the spiritual bondage we often face. The enemy's strategy is to remind us of who we were, to convince us that freedom is unattainable. Consider the Medes and the Scythians. When the Medes revolted, the Scythians stopped fighting with weapons and came armed only with whips. The sight of those whips reminded the Medes of their status as slaves, and they fled. Similarly, Satan uses our past, fears, and weaknesses to keep us enslaved. He whispers, "You'll never be free," or "You're not worthy of God's promises."

But the truth is, God doesn't call perfect people. He calls the broken, the weary, and the burdened. When God called the Israelites, they weren't a mighty nation; they were a struggling group of people with baggage, pain, and fear. Yet God saw their potential, just as He sees yours.

The Israelites approached the Jordan River and were on the brink of the Promised Land. They had left Egypt behind, but stepping into their destiny meant facing new challenges. Destiny is stepping into the unknown at times. This is true in all forms of walking with God, ministry, finances, relationships. In order to have what God has for us we must take it and deal with what would hinder us. Crossing over wasn't just about geography; it was about mindset.

Many Christians today find themselves in a similar place. They've been saved, but they haven't fully embraced the freedom and purpose God has for them. Fear of the unknown holds them back—fear of failure, giants, fear of the Jordan River standing in their way.

David never knew that his destiny was on the other side of Goliath. Yet, had he let fear paralyze him, he would have missed the fulfillment of God's plan. What is your "giant" today? What obstacle stands between you and the life God has called you to?

Often, we hesitate because we feel the weight of responsibility. We think it all depends on us, forgetting that God is the one who goes before us. Proverbs 20:24 reminds us,

> ***"A man's steps are of the Lord; how can a man understand his own way?"***

One of the most powerful tools God gave the Israelites at the Jordan was the command to set up twelve stones as a testimony. These stones weren't just rocks but a declaration of God's faithfulness.

When future generations asked, "What do these stones mean?" the Israelites responded, "This is where God dried up the Jordan so we could cross on dry land." It was a tangible reminder of God's power and provision—a way to declare, "If He did it, then He can do it again."

In our lives, we need to set up our own "stones" of testimony. These are moments where we remind ourselves and others of God's faithfulness. Perhaps it's how He healed you, restored your marriage, or brought you out of despair. Whatever it is, it's a weapon against the enemy's lies.

I'll never forget when I was a new convert, and the enemy attacked my mind. I didn't feel like I belonged in church. Surrounded by happy people, At 17 years old I felt out of place and left. As I stood outside a liquor store waiting for a guy to grab me a quart of Mickey's beer, an old woman from church followed me and picked me up. She reminded me of God's truth. That moment became a testimony—a stone I carry to this day.

The Jordan River wasn't just an obstacle; it was a marker. On one side was a history of slavery and wandering, and on the other was a future filled with promise. Crossing the Jordan meant leaving behind the past and embracing a new identity as God's chosen people.

The Jordan often represents the barriers in our lives that keep us from stepping into God's best. It's easy to stay on the "safe" side, where things are familiar but unfulfilling. But God calls us to something greater. He calls us to step into the unknown, trusting that He has prepared the way. Remember, God is always at work, even when we can't see it. Like the woman who planted flowers and because they were taking too long to grow she was going to kill them. Right before she was going to use a shovel her neighbor yelled thanking her for the beautifying the neighborhood. When she looked on the other side of her wall she found them blooming on the other side. She went off of what she couldn't see. We may not realize how God orchestrates things for our good even though we don't see it..

Destiny requires action. It means taking steps of faith, praying boldly, and believing that God can do the impossible.

As Paul said, *"I press toward the goal for the prize of the upward call of God in Christ Jesus"* (Philippians 3:14).

The Israelites' journey to the Promised Land wasn't without struggle, but it was worth it. The same is true for you. God is calling you to embark on your destiny, to leave behind the chains of the past, and to step into a future filled with His promises. There is a real Call for you to cross over.

What is holding you back today? What "Jordan River" do you need to cross? Remember, God is on the other side, waiting to show you, His faithfulness. Take the step. Embrace your destiny. The land of promise is closer than you think.

By Joshua L Neal

3. Embracing Destiny:
When God's Plan Becomes Our Own

Destiny isn't stumbled upon; it's embraced. It requires intentional choices that align with God's purpose for our lives. This truth is vividly seen in the story of Moses, a man who faced pivotal decisions that shaped not only his own life but also the destiny of an entire nation. The journey of embracing destiny begins with the decisions we make, the faith we hold, and the paths we choose to walk.

The life of Moses is a powerful example of how embracing destiny begins with saying "no" to what the world offers and "yes" to God. Born into a unique position of privilege as the adopted son of Pharaoh's daughter, Moses had every opportunity to enjoy wealth, power, and prominence. Moses could have chosen the easier way in life. Yet, the Bible records a remarkable decision:

> *"By faith Moses, when he became of age, refused to be called the son of Pharaoh's daughter, choosing rather to suffer affliction with the people of God than to enjoy the passing pleasures of sin,*

By Joshua L Neal

> *esteeming the reproach of Christ greater riches than the treasures in Egypt; for he looked to the reward."* —Hebrews 11:24–26

Moses could have played it safe. He could have enjoyed the best of both worlds: the treasures of Egypt and the knowledge of God. But destiny doesn't thrive on divided loyalty. Moses understood a vital truth: you cannot play both sides of the fence. To embrace the fullness of God's purpose, he had to leave behind the comforts of Egypt and align himself with God's people.

It's tempting to ask, "*Can I enjoy the world and still walk in the will of God?*" But Moses teaches us that double-mindedness only leads to instability and sorrow. Like someone caught between two options, constantly pulled in different directions, a double-minded person is left unsteady and unable to move forward in faith. James speaks about wisdom regarding this and shows us that it takes some wisdom not to be double-minded. James 1:5–8 (NKJV)5 If any of you lacks wisdom, let him ask of God, who gives to all liberally and without reproach, and it will be given to him. 6 But let him ask in faith, with no doubting, for he who doubts is like a wave of the sea driven and tossed by the wind. 7 For let not that man suppose that he will receive anything from the Lord; 8 he is a double-minded man, unstable in all his ways.

So, Moses' decision to walk away from Pharaoh's palace was not an easy one. Think about what it meant: leaving the wealth, comfort, and security of royal life for the uncertainty of the wilderness. It seemed like a step backward. Who would willingly trade a palace for a tent or royal feasts for manna in the desert? A nice empire for a pile of dirt?

Yet Moses understood something more profound: the riches of Egypt were temporary, but the reward of obeying God was eternal. His faith gave him the spiritual grit to choose the more arduous path because he trusted God's plan.

It's a lesson we can all learn from. How often are we tempted to settle for less because it feels safe? How frequently do we resist stepping out in faith because we fear losing what we already have? Moses reminds us that sometimes embracing destiny requires us to take what looks like a step backward to move forward in God's plan.

As Psalm 84:10 says:

> ***"For a day in Your courts is better than a thousand. I would rather be a doorkeeper in the house of my God than dwell in the tents of wickedness."***

One of the most significant obstacles to embracing destiny is poor decision-making. Many people miss God's plan for their lives because they choose what feels right in the moment rather than seeking God's will. The story of Jonah serves as a warning: when God called Jonah to go to Nineveh, he decided to flee to Tarshish instead. Go to the hot and dry Nineveh or hang out in Spain. Jonah decided that Spain was a much better option. Jonah's disobedience didn't just delay his destiny—it endangered his life and the lives of those around him.

Proverbs 14:12 reminds us:

> ***"There is a way that seems right to a man, but its end is the way of death."***

God often whispers His will into our hearts, prompting us through the Holy Spirit. Yet, how frequently do we resist God dealing with our hearts? How frequently do we allow fear, distractions, or the influence of others to hinder us from following His direction? The Apostle Paul warns us in Galatians 5:7:

> ***"You ran well. Who hindered you from obeying the truth?"***

To embrace destiny, we must learn to listen to the voice of the Holy Spirit and trust His guidance. Just as God gave Moses clear instructions—"Take off your shoes," "Stretch out your hand," "Set my people free"—He will direct our steps if we are willing to follow. Embracing God's destiny means we are open and willing to allow God to change our minds and conform our will to his will.

By Joshua L Neal

4. Obtaining Destiny: <u>The Journey To God's Promise</u>

Destiny isn't handed to us on a silver platter. It doesn't arrive wrapped in a bow with applause from the world. Instead, it must be desired, pursued, and obtained through faith, perseverance, and sacrifice. Jacob's story teaches us that obtaining destiny requires navigating setbacks, overcoming frustrations, and making intentional choices to walk in God's will. Though the path may be challenging, the rewards are eternal and deeply fulfilling. I was raised in a rough neighborhood. This neighborhood was called the Camino de Jacobo County Projects. In English, it is Jacob's Way County Projects. Our neighborhood definitely had the spirit of Jacob. We learned how to steal, lie, and cheat each other from an early age. Jacob, who is known as a heel grabber who cheated his brother, would have fit just fine in our neighborhood. Like many of us, Jacob had to learn about destiny through the school of hard knocks.

Jacob's journey begins with a desire for something greater. He had seized his brother Esau's birthright and blessing—albeit through deception—because he wanted what Esau despised. This speaks to an essential truth: destiny doesn't fall into our laps; we must desire it.

However, many of us have a flawed expectation of the road to destiny. In our minds, it's a smooth, pleasant path free of obstacles or opposition. But the reality is far from this idealized picture. Jacob's own life at this point was anything but glamorous. He was running for his life, a vagabond fleeing his brother's wrath. The Bible paints a vivid picture of his situation:

> ***"So, he came to a certain place and stayed there all night because the sun had set. And he took one of the stones of that place and put it at his head and lay down to sleep."***— Genesis 28:11

Jacob's circumstances were far from ideal. He didn't have a red carpet rolled out for him or anyone applauding his choices. Similarly, when deciding to pursue God's will, we may find that people come against us or try to discourage us. Even Jesus faced this when His family questioned His path. Yet He pressed on, understanding that the journey to destiny often comes with sacrifice and misunderstanding. The sad truth is we care too much about what people think.

One of the most significant challenges in obtaining destiny is overcoming the frustrations that arise along the way. These frustrations can cause us to question the sacrifices we've made and the decisions we've committed to for God. We may ask: "If this is God's will, why am I struggling? Why does this path feel so hard?"

Jacob's journey was full of ups and downs. His choices often led to detours and delays, like the years he spent working for Laban, only to be deceived repeatedly. Yet even in these frustrating moments, Jacob remained on the path to God's promise. The Bible doesn't say but I wonder about the moments where Jacob sat and contemplated his life's choices. His choices isolated himself from his family. He could have continued on the downward spiral of bad choices and devastating consequences. However, what the Bible does show us is that Jacob made a decision to live differently.

Destiny is not a utopian ideal. Destiny is not perfection without pitfalls. Often it is messing up and getting back up again. It's a process that refines and shapes us into the people God has called us to be. Jesus Himself reminded His disciples of this reality:

> "*Foxes have holes, and birds of the air have nests, but the Son of Man has nowhere to lay His head.*"—Matthew 8:20

Jesus is saying *"Listen up there will hard times if you come with me. Birds and foxes have places of coziness but I am furthering the Kingdom of God even if it means I am uncomfortable. Some believers get frustrated and wonder how the will of God could be uncomfortable and frustrating. Setbacks and frustrations are not signs that God's will has failed. Instead, they are opportunities for growth and reminders to trust in God's faithfulness."*

Amid Jacob's frustrations, something extraordinary happens: God meets him. As Jacob lies asleep with a stone for a pillow, he dreams of a ladder reaching heaven, with angels ascending and descending on it. At the top of the ladder stands the Lord, who speaks these words of promise:

> "***I am the Lord God of Abraham your father and the God of Isaac; the land on which you lie I will give to you and your descendants. ... Behold, I am with you and will keep you wherever you go, and will bring you back to this land; for I will not leave you until I have done what I have spoken to you.***"—Genesis 28:13-15

This divine encounter reminds Jacob—and us—that even in our most challenging moments, God is present. Sometimes, we need a supernatural reminder of our calling. It's easy to hear and grow numb to God's promises, especially when the path to fulfillment feels uncertain. God decided to remind Jacob through an MMA match. There was back-and-forth fighting. God would get the upper hand, and then Jacob would. This sounds a lot like how we function in God's will. God deals, we obey and then fight him at every turn. However, God is longsuffering, as we shall see. God takes the time to continue with us. When God reminds us of His plans, it reignites our faith and passion for Him.

Why does God continue to help us, even when we falter? Because He is a God of destiny. He desires to see His purposes fulfilled in our lives, not because we are perfect, but because He loves us and delights in unfolding His plans. God allows us to play a small part in His overall plan. Do you think that God couldn't open the Red Sea without Moses? Of course, God could have done it without Moses. God desires to move through us as His chosen instruments.

Jacob's persistence in wrestling with God demonstrates this truth. He didn't quit or give up on his destiny, even when it seemed out of reach. For those who feel like our calling has been sidelined or forgotten, Jacob's story is a challenge to reengage with our destiny. It's time to wrestle with God again and pursue the promises He has spoken over our lives.

Jacob received revelation in the will of God. Jacob can pass these four decisions down to us:

#1 He immediately honored God in tithes

#2 After his encounter with God, Jacob declares, "This is none other than the house of God, and this is the gate of heaven!" He names the place Bethel, meaning "house of God." This signifies the importance of the church and God's design for the community. Destiny is not fulfilled in isolation—it is cultivated through fellowship and service within the body of Christ.

#3 Jacob sacrifices his comfort to have a destiny - Turns a pillow into an altar!

#4 Surrenders his will to God's will - He recognizes God's Kingship

The journey to destiny is not without its challenges but is deeply fulfilling. As Paul writes: "Eye has not seen, nor ear heard, nor have entered into the heart of man the things which God has prepared for those who love Him."—1 Corinthians 2:9

Jacob's story reminds us that setbacks and frustrations are part of the process, but God is faithful to His promises. He will meet, guide, and empower us to fulfill the destiny He has prepared for us. It is amazing to think that the greatest gift God desires in accomplishing His purposes in the world is us. Pastor Greg Mitchell some years back preached a sermon at the Door Church in Chandler. He used the illustration of a little boy who was moved by God in the service when the offering plate was passed and he had nothing to give. When the offering plate came to him. He put it on the ground and stood inside of it offering himself. This is a wonderful picture of what God really wants. It is us and our will aligning with his.

Pastor Wayman Mitchell said the greatest miracle is when man's will and God's will come into alignment. We can have destiny when we surrender and have our nevertheless not my will but thy will.

Now is the time to desire destiny, pursue it with all your heart, and make the choices that bring you closer to God. Destiny isn't just a dream—it's a reality waiting to be obtained by those willing to walk the path of faith. Will you take the first step today?

5. Destiny In Babylon:
Character Counts

A wise man once said, "Wherever you go, there you are." This simple truth speaks volumes about the human condition. Often, we believe that if we can change our environment, we can change our lives. But the reality is this: our character follows us no matter where we go. I was getting into trouble at 17 years old and it wasn't getting better no matter how many times I told my mother I would change. I had the bright idea that if I was going to change myself then I would go to Tennessee to live with my father. When I arrived, there was a six-pack of beer and a pack of cigarettes waiting for me. I thought if I left my friends I would be leaving the temptation to sin. However, When I walked into my father's house sin was already waiting for me. I never said no to my sin because I had a bad character and when I showed up in Tennessee there, I was the same bound individual with my chains of addiction. Escaping a lousy climate doesn't mean we escape the person we've become. Daniel's story in Babylon reminds us that destiny sometimes isn't about location—it's about who we are when everything around us tries to change us. Remember if it was up to Daniel he would be in Israel and not in Babylon. The will of God has a location and an address. Jesus sets members in the body (church) as it pleases Him. However, Daniel was taken by force yet still able to live for God.

One of the problems is that there is a real dilemma with our environment. We come to a service, and God powerfully moves us by His Spirit, and we surrender, recognizing our sins. However, unless you live in the church, your environment changes, and for many, it is like Babylon. An environment where others are not too excited about your new life and your new God. This new environment wherever it is in the world wants to watch who you really bow down to. I had family members tell me that they loved me more when I was drunk or high. If we don't understand these words can really affect us.

It's indisputable that environments affect us. Research shows that the atmosphere we live in—whether physical, emotional, or spiritual—can mold our mood, decisions, and even our faith. Hospitals know this; studies reveal that patients recover faster in bright, peaceful environments than in dark, dreary ones. The opposite is also true. Saddam Hussein would put his prisoners in a room that was painted red and after days in this room prisoners would go crazy. He didn't abuse them physically sometimes but would just change their environment and madness would set in.

So, while environments can uplift, they can also corrupt. They create dynamics that challenge our walk with God. Job's accuser understood this when he questioned Job's ability to serve God if his environment turned harsh or dry:

> ***"Can the papyrus grow up without a marsh? Can the reeds flourish without water?"*** (Job 8:11).

The message is clear even with Job's not so great friends. They understood a truth about how our atmosphere can affect our faith. In other words, our environment can nurture or choke our faith.

Babylon was designed to reshape people. It didn't just capture nations; it captured identities. Daniel and his friends faced this firsthand. Their Hebrew names, rich with godly meaning, were stripped away and replaced with names glorifying Babylonian gods. Daniel became Belteshazzar, a name proclaiming "Bel will protect" or "favored by Bel" or "Bel's Prince" in honor of the god Baal.

The food they were given wasn't just a meal but a declaration. The meat and wine were first offered to the gods of Babylon, symbolizing that their new masters were the providers. The message was clear: You belong to us now.

Many of us face our own Babylon. Whether it's a toxic workplace, societal pressure, the media, or our culture has an agenda—a direction it's moving toward, often hidden in plain sight. Babylon seeks to erode our convictions and conform us to its image. Our Babylon's might be bad relationships we keep. We can be affected by our old friends who mock and scorn what God is trying to do in our lives. The old saying is true "If you lie down with dogs you'll wake up with fleas." I preached a sermon in Blythe CA and made a quick comment that when we are saved, we should get rid of the drug dealers phone number. It is sad to see what people hold on to.

Daniel didn't choose Babylon; he was forced into it because of Israel's disobedience. Yet, in the middle of this hostile environment, Daniel sowed into his character: "Daniel purposed in his heart that he would not defile himself with the portion of the king's delicacies." (Daniel 1:8)

Daniel knew that character begins with small decisions. As the saying goes:

> ***"Sow a thought, reap an act; sow an act, reap a habit; sow a habit, reap a character; sow a character, reap a destiny."***

Our environment may challenge us, but it doesn't have to define us. Blaming our surroundings is easy, but true transformation begins when we take responsibility for our choices. One man said, "An Englishman is English wherever he goes." Let this be said about us: "A Christian is a Christian wherever he goes." Matthew Henry said it best: "Wherever a good man goes, he desires to take God along."

Daniel's greatest strength was his unshakable character. He didn't need a spiritual pep rally or a supportive crowd to do what was right. In the heart of a sinful city, surrounded by temptation, Daniel purposed in his heart to please God. In other words Daniel made God his audience.

The Bible teaches us not to conform to our surroundings: "Do not be conformed to this world, but be transformed by the renewing of your mind." - Romans 12:2

Daniel's inner renewal allowed him to resist the external pressures of Babylon. He didn't justify compromise, even when it would have been easy. Like Joseph, who resisted Potiphar's wife despite being a slave, Daniel chose righteousness over convenience and compromise.

Compromise often begins inwardly. Proverbs warns us:

> **"*For as he thinks in his heart, so is he.*"** - Proverbs 23:7

The battle for character is fought and won in our thoughts. What we entertain in our minds will eventually manifest in our actions. Bad company, ungodly influences, and toxic atmospheres are like seeds of compromise. As Paul wrote: "Do not be deceived: 'Evil company corrupts good habits.'" - 1 Corinthians 15:33

Daniel guarded his heart and mind, refusing to let Babylon corrupt his convictions. This is done when we decide to make God our audience, not man. Pastor Mitchell had a quote that he would start off with a question. "What do you do when you don't know what to do?" Then he would answer with "Keep doing what you know to do." This is very practical wisdom that can keep our hearts right when there are sirens singing out for us to do wrong in our society.

Lot who was Abraham's nephew lived in Sodom and Gomorrah and his soul was vexed because of this ungodly environment.

"7 And delivered just Lot, vexed with the filthy conversation of the wicked: 8 (For that righteous man dwelling among them, in seeing and hearing, vexed his righteous soul from day to day with their unlawful deeds;" - 2 Peter 2:7-8

It was Daniel's integrity that protected his own destiny and inspired others. His faithfulness encouraged his friends—Shadrach, Meshach, and Abednego—to stand firm, even when faced with a fiery furnace.

Daniel's secret was his relationship with God. He prayed three times a day, even when it was illegal. He opened his windows toward Jerusalem, showing his heart for God's people and purposes. Prayer aligned Daniel's heart with God's, giving him the strength to stand firm.

When we pray consistently, we begin to care about what God cares about. This alignment transforms us and enables us to convert others. This wasn't a show or some performance but because Daniel truly needed God and he desired God's presence and power in his life. As a new convert I had some buddies bragging one time about who woke up the earliest to pray. This was said with the idea that if you get up earlier you must be holier than others. As you mature in the faith and develop some Christian character your prayer life becomes absolutely necessary for survival. You will never rise above your prayer life. Showing up to pray is just creating the atmosphere to have an encounter with God. We can become like the Pharisee in Jesus' parable who "prayed thus with himself." He became a religious man whose prayer stopped touching heaven. Which also explains his lack of concern for the lost man who is praying next to him. Alan Redpath said it best when he said "Some men are so heavenly minded they are of no earthly value." When we pray because it's just what we do we are in danger. Religious practices without heart always produces the worst examples of the faith. Spiritual routines without a heart for God creates lemmings without convictions. It is more than just doing what we do as believers it is becoming like who He is.

Daniel's unwavering character prepared him for the lion's den. He didn't develop courage overnight; it was built daily, decision by decision, in the small moments of obedience. Jesus said it perfectly when he said:

> *"He who is faithful in what is least is faithful also in much, and he who is unjust in what is least is unjust also in much."* Luke 16:10 (NKJV)

Because Daniel stood firm in Babylon, he could stand in the lions' den—and God delivered him. His faithfulness didn't just save his life; it changed a nation. King Darius proclaimed to all his people: "For He is the living God, and steadfast forever; His kingdom is the one which shall not be destroyed, and His dominion shall endure to the end." (Daniel 6:26)

Daniel's character didn't just affect him; it influenced a king, a nation, and countless generations. The same is true for us. Who's watching how you live for God? Whose destiny hinges on your faithfulness?

Character isn't just about personal growth—it's about fulfilling our God-given destiny and inspiring others to do the same. Remember it is in the daily obedience's that are seen by nobody else except God. When we allow God to fashion and shape us through changing our character more and more into His image fruit will follow. The seeds of living right will begin to sprout and grow strong in our lives. This must be done with a heart of integrity. What is integrity? It is who you are when no one is watching. It is the daily decisions that we know would make God happy.

One day, the well-known preacher Clovis Chappell sat with two friends, discussing the challenges of life's journey. He posed a simple yet profound question: "What do you think is the hardest part of any journey?"

The first friend thought for a moment and confidently answered, "The beginning! That's when the fear of the unknown sets in, and taking that first step can feel overwhelming."

But the second friend shook his head and disagreed. "No, the beginning is exciting! That's when you're fresh, full of energy, and eager to move forward. I believe the hardest part is the end—when exhaustion sets in, and you're struggling to take the final steps."

Chappell smiled, listening intently, then leaned in and said, "You're both wrong. The hardest part of any journey is the middle."

His friends looked at him, puzzled.

"Why the middle?" one of them asked.

With wisdom in his voice, Chappell explained, "Because at the start, you have excitement. At the end, you have the finish line in sight. But in the middle, there is no one there to cheer you on. That's when doubt creeps in, when fatigue begins to weigh you down, and when the temptation to turn back is strongest."

His words hung in the air like a revelation. The middle of the journey—whether in life, faith, or personal struggles—is where perseverance is tested. It is in the unseen moments, when no one is watching, that true endurance is forged.

In the face of Babylon's pressures, Daniel showed us that character counts. Destiny isn't determined by our environment but by our response to it. Like Daniel, we are called to stand firm, live by conviction, and please God no matter where we are.

Who knows what God will do through your life if you purpose in your heart to honor Him? Stand strong. Your destiny, and the destiny of others, depends on it.

Let me ask you two questions:

1. Where are you at right now?
2. How's your environment?

By Joshua L Neal

6. Examined Destiny:
Examining The Soul Of True Discipleship

Some years ago, a book was written titled *Autopsy of a Deceased Church* by Thom Rainer. His book was about asking churches questions trying to figure out why some churches die. I believe in this chapter we should consider an "autopsy of a deceased disciple." Like decorative vases that come with a disclaimer inside them stating that their inner quality cannot be guaranteed, so too do many disciples look the part outwardly but lack the necessary inner transformation. As 1 Samuel 16:7 reminds us:

> *"Man looks at the outward appearance, but the Lord looks at the heart."*

We witness Jesus and His disciples at the Last Supper. The solemn moment unfolds as Jesus reveals that one of them will betray Him. Their sorrowful responses, "Lord, is it I?" reflect the gravity of discipleship and the condition of the heart.

When evening had come, He sat down with the twelve. Now as they were eating, He said, "Assuredly, I say to you, one of you will betray Me."

And they were exceedingly sorrowful, and each of them began to say to Him, "Lord, is it I?" He answered and said, *"He who dipped his hand with Me in the dish will betray Me. The Son of Man indeed goes just as it is written of Him, but woe to that man by whom the Son of Man is betrayed! It would have been good for that man if he had not been born."* Then Judas, who was betraying Him, answered and said, "Rabbi, is it I?" He said to him, "You have said it." - Matthew 26:20-25 NKJV

This somber scene even begins with "When evening had come." The atmosphere here would have been intense. In v22 "They were exceedingly sorrowful…" The reason for this sorrow is because Jesus knew one of them would betray him. One of the disciples is going astray. This pain would have been really bad for Jesus and the disciples. Betrayal is never easy but it hurts when it is by those closest to you. In fact, the Bible prophesies about the pain Jesus would feel at this moment in ministry!

And one will say to him, 'What are these wounds between your arms?' Then he will answer, 'Those with which I was wounded in the house of my friends.' - Zechariah 13:6 (NKJV). The truth is that Jesus had been hurt by many in life and ministry. The Pharisees, Sadducees and then later by his own family. If you are a reader of history there are many chapters that include betrayal. Julias Caesar when he recognizes that Brutus his dear friend was amongst the assassins, he drops his hands and quits fighting back with the famous words of "Et tu Brute?" Leonardo Di Vinci captures betrayal in his famous painting of the last supper with Judas knocking over the salt with his left elbow. Rice is put in salt shakers because salt is so accustomed to sticking together. This is a picture of fellowship.

Pastor Mitchell had to deal with numerous betrayals in the Kingdom of God. One time on the way to the airport he told me a story about how some rebellious men pulled churches out of our fellowship. These were men he had invested in. To be betrayed by your own disciples is hard to bare because it is contrary to what has been taught. In his kitchen Pastor Mitchell said "If this is what is going to happen when I launch men then I'm not doing it." God spoke to Pastor Mitchell's heart and said "You do what I have called you to do." Paul the Apostle was also betrayed and he writes in a letter addressed to Timothy chapter 4 verse 10 "And Demas has forsaken me."

When we read about Jesus in this room during the last supper, we can assume that Jesus was unconcerned for Judas. I have heard quite a few sermons on how Judas was being rebuked by Jesus. However, when I read this, I clearly believe that Jesus was making this all obvious in an attempt to win Judas back. When we are betrayed usually, we want to strike back in some way. This is not who Jesus is. Jesus sees past the dumb decisions. Jesus knows where bad decisions can take us out. In fact, later Jesus warned Peter about betrayal. Also, here I believe Jesus was trying to reach Judas. Remember that Jesus saw potential in Judas. Jesus discipled Judas for three years. There was an impartation of spirit. Judas cast out demons, laid hands on the sick, and saw the dead raised.

The question is how does a disciple go from functioning in the power of God, winning souls and seeing miracles to betraying Jesus. Where did Judas go wrong? One man said "Backsliding is never a blowout but it is usually a slow leak." The Judas' problem was a problem in the heart. His ministry started to define who he was. His success and privilege made him feel entitled. He became a professional disciple. He quoted Jesus, maybe used the same hand gestures while he taught like Jesus. He had the mechanics of a disciple but didn't have the Fathers heart! Remember the elder son in Jesus' parable of the prodigal. The elder son lived in his father's house with privilege but he didn't have the father's heart for his lost brother.

Judas' heart is revealed in our text. When Jesus brings up betrayal the other disciples in V22 say "Lord is it I?" The word Lord is the Greek word "kurios" which means possessor of all I am while Judas uses "Master is it I?" The word master seems reverent however, it is the Greek word "Rhabi" which means "only a teacher."

The problem here is that Judas never crossed over from Jesus being his teacher to Jesus his Lord. The question is how does someone do this? How do they miss the Lordship of Jesus? The sad reality is that a disciple who drifts off like Judas has to minimize who Jesus is. It's like dying in the hospital because you never checked in at the desk. Sitting in the hospital's waiting room won't heal you because your vitals were never checked. You never allowed the physician to make his diagnosis and offer healing. It is the same as believers. I went to church! I was involved! However, Jesus was never given his place in your life as Lord. In other words, you sat in a church but never had your spiritual vitals checked by the great physician. Paul the Apostle had to ask older saints:

> ***"Examine yourselves as to whether you are in the faith. Test yourselves. Do you not know yourselves, that Jesus Christ is in you? —unless indeed you are disqualified."***
> - 2 Corinthians 13:5 (NKJV)

There are some reasons why Judas might have meandered off to a backslidden state. He was from Keturah which would have been more of a bustling town. In Galilee the disciples would have known each other and they might have assimilated a little bit better. If he was already an outsider, he might have started to isolate himself. Did Judas have a spirit of rejection? Who knows for sure. Did the devil show him that he was an outsider? Possibly.

Judas did two things. #1 He came to the place where he said no to Jesus' Lordship. This was very foolish. Remember the warning in the Bible: The fool has said in his heart, "There is no God." - Psalm 14:1 (NKJV) - "There is" in in italics actual reading is:

"The fool has said in this heart no God."

#2 Judas minimized Jesus in his life. He minimized Jesus so much that Jesus was only worth 30 pieces of silver. Judas made the statement that Jesus was worth less than money. His greed began to rule his life. In other words, Mammon became his new god.

> *"No one can serve two masters; for either he will hate the one and love the other, or else he will be loyal to the one and despise the other. You cannot serve God and mammon."*
> -Matthew 6:24 (NKJV)

Think about the privilege and trust that was placed on Judas who possibly already has an issue with greed. Jesus gives him the money bags. Jesus wanted Judas to have dominion in all areas of ministry.

The ultimate plan of the enemy is to sow seeds of isolation and rejection so you stay away from your headship and God. I used to watch the old animal documentaries that show lions chasing gazelles in Africa. We would naturally think that because lions are so big and strong they would go after a strong gazelle. However, this is not the case in many instances. Lions actually prefer the young or really old gazelle that is isolate or too weak to get away. The devil is the same way. He goes after the weak or the isolated one. In fact, the enemy is always searching for these types of believers.

> ***Be sober, be vigilant; because your adversary the devil walks about like a roaring lion, seeking whom he may devour.***
> - 1 Peter 5:8 (NKJV)

Remember Jesus is fully God and fully man or he couldn't be a full redeemer between God and man.

Pastor Greg Mitchell spoke some words in one of his sermons that I have never forgotten "Rejected people reject people." This is absolutely true in my own life. If I ever felt like I was going to receive rejection I would immediately write people off. This was something I learned from my own mother. She would have a friend one day and the next day never speak to them again. This is unhealthy for life. Was it possible that Judas faced rejection when Jesus rebuked him for his comments? Let's read it.

> *"And being in Bethany at the house of Simon the leper, as He sat at the table, a woman came having an alabaster flask of very costly oil of spikenard. Then she broke the flask and poured it on His head. But there were some who were indignant among themselves, and said, "Why was this fragrant oil wasted? For it might have been sold for more than three hundred denarii and given to the poor." And they criticized her sharply. But Jesus said, "Let her alone. Why do you trouble her? She has done a good work for Me."* - Mark 14:3–6 (NKJV)

It is right after this that Judas runs off to sell Jesus. The bible says that all the disciples made this comment but it seems as if Judas processed Jesus' correction differently. Again, Pastor Greg in my discipleship has said in teaching and correcting disciples "I am not rejecting you as a person but what you're doing. Today it is small issues but later in ministry souls and people can be affected." The sad reality is you can be saved and a disciple functioning in ministry and still feel as if you don't belong. Correction has always been intended to bring us closer to God in relationship. However, since Adam and Eve correction processed incorrectly has always driven us further away from God.

It is interesting that Peter is rebuked a number of times but he processed it differently. Jesus told Peter "Get behind me Satan." Whether Peter was called Satan or the words he spoke were the words of Satan, this rebuke is rough to read. However, Peter kept going and defended Jesus on the night of Jesus' betrayal and arrest until he didn't. He misunderstood in swinging his sword.

Peter gives us one of the greatest examples of discipleship. He was one who said "Lord is it I?" So, those who said that Jesus possessed them made it. Yes, Peter denied, cussed and hid but he was restored again. Jesus gives us the answer for how we can examine our destiny in discipleship. Remember Jesus shows up on the shore when the disciples were fishing and Peter jumps into the water first to get to Jesus. Let's look:

> ***So, when they had eaten breakfast, Jesus said to Simon Peter, "Simon, son of Jonah, do you love Me more than these?" He said to Him, "Yes, Lord; You know that I love You." He said to him, "Feed My lambs." 16He said to him again a second time, "Simon, son of Jonah, do you love Me?" He said to Him, "Yes, Lord; You know that I love You." He said to him, "Tend My sheep."***

> *17He said to him the third time, "Simon, son of Jonah, do you love Me?" Peter was grieved because He said to him the third time, "Do you love Me?" And he said to Him, "Lord, You know all things; You know that I love You." Jesus said to him, "Feed My sheep.* -John 21:15–17 (NKJV)

Jesus doesn't berate Peter. Jesus doesn't say that Peter was dumb. Jesus doesn't say that Peter was a big waste of three years of discipleship. Jesus simply brings Peter to the starting point of discipleship. Love God with all your heart. Jesus shows Peter that you can have all the mechanics of ministry and not be motivated by love. Remember Jesus' words:

> *"Not everyone who says to Me, 'Lord, Lord,' shall enter the kingdom of heaven, but he who does the will of My Father in heaven. 22Many will say to Me in that day, 'Lord, Lord, have we not prophesied in Your name, cast out demons in Your name, and done many wonders in Your name?' And then I will declare to them, 'I never knew you; depart from Me, you who practice lawlessness!'"*-Matthew 7:21–23 (NKJV)

Love is the real issue as to why someone can sell out their calling for cash, car, and career. This is why sometimes relationships are chosen over calling. Why? Because when you love God there is nothing you wouldn't do for Him. When someone loves God, you don't have to ask them to be faithful. They tithe, change in character, treat people right. What is powerful here though is that it is not in how much we love God but in how much He loves us. When you get the revelation of God's love, fear and rejection dissipate.

I was reading a Christian book in my living room that had nothing to do with the love of God and I can't explain it but I received the revelation that God really does love me. I wept when I felt God's presence. Why did God show up for me that way? I guess because He can, He is God.

Maybe you are reading this and struggling in your walk with God. Maybe struggling in your discipleship. Maybe you're being lied to by the enemy. The truth is you can experience God's love. The old saying is true "Religion will put a new suit on a man but only relationship with God will put a new man in the suit." It is interesting that Judas was a vessel refusing to be formed by Jesus and he commits suicide in the Potters field with all the other discarded broken vessels. Like decorative vases that come with a disclaimer inside them stating that their inner quality cannot be guaranteed. The truth is for us we can choose to have inner quality. We can be a disciple who speaks and lives truth inwardly and outwardly.

Do not let your heartless discipleship destroy the destiny God had for you. I have heard a story from a pastor who went to Jerusalem with Pastor Mitchell. He told me that he knew they were at the potter's field because of all the broken shards of pottery left around. This pastor said that the pottery was still breaking under his feet while he walked around there. The truth is if we don't allow God to mold us and put us into the fire to be tried and strengthened in His love we can become a discarded vessel. God has called you to make an impact in the earth for the Kingdom of God. This means you have to decide to allow God to become the possessor of all your being. Not in the verbiage of words but in truth. God can heal your rejection and show you, His love.

1. Have you searched for your own internal flaws and worked them out with Jesus?
2. Remember it is always better to be right rather than looking right.

By Joshua L Neal

7. Fruitful Destiny: <u>Destined To Bear Fruit</u>

The Tomatoes in the Sinkhole illustrates what I want to encourage you with in this chapter. In the city of Toronto, something remarkable happened. A massive sinkhole became a symbol of community resilience. Frustrated residents, tired of waiting for city officials to repair the hole, planted tomato seeds in its depths. Against all odds, the seeds flourished. The tomatoes grew tall and healthy, tended by neighbors who had every reason to see the sinkhole as a problem—but instead saw an opportunity. Eventually, the tomatoes were moved to a community garden, where they would thrive even further.

This story is a picture of how destiny can flourish in the most unexpected places. Like the tomatoes, we often find ourselves planted in the middle of a mess, unsure of what will come next. But when we view our circumstances through God's lens, we see His hand at work, preparing us for something greater.

The Israelites in Numbers 14 had a divine destiny ahead. The Promised Land! This land wasn't just any territory—it was a place of abundance, a land flowing with milk and honey. But as we know, milk and honey don't flow out of the ground on their own. They require effort. God's promises often come with projects, and His blessings come with responsibility.

This land was more than a material blessing; it was a spiritual haven. It represented a place where families could flourish, where marriages could thrive, and where people could worship freely. It was a destiny marked by both physical and spiritual abundance.

But despite the richness of God's promise, the Israelites were hindered—not by an outward enemy but by their own perspective. The spies sent by Moses brought back a negative report, and instead of seeing the land's potential, they focused on its challenges.

How often do we do the same? We sing a song in our churches called "Who's report will you believe? We shall believe the report of the Lord." It matters what we believe because what we believe can help or hurt destiny. God places opportunities in front of us, but instead of seeing the possibilities, we focus on the obstacles. We let fear and unbelief shape our view of God's plan for us, missing the greatness He has prepared.

What are these hinderances of unbelief? When we become cynical in the Kingdom of God our destiny is soured and becomes a chore.

Cynical unbelief is one of the greatest enemies of destiny. It's contagious and often louder than faith. The ten spies infected the entire congregation with their doubt. They allowed fear to dominate their thoughts, and as a result, the people rejected God's promise.

Jesus Himself encountered this spirit of unbelief. In Mark 5:39–40, when He came to heal a girl thought to be dead, the crowd ridiculed Him. But Jesus removed the doubters and performed the miracle. Sometimes, we must push past the noise of unbelief to see God's hand move. In other words, Jesus changed the atmosphere from cynical doubt to faith. Faith triggers faith. Pastor Wayman Mitchell and Pastor Greg will preach a short message on faith and then will even call up some people that need smaller healings and this triggers faith for some of the greater miracles and healings that God would do in a healing crusade. A negative example of this was one time in my church I was closing the service but God dealt with my heart to pray for people before I closed. In fact, God did more than that he spoke about certain illness in particular that needed healing. God was moving and some new converts were healed. God told me that there was a man who needed healing on a tooth on his lower left side in the back. It turned out to be a visitor. This visitor was blown away because he didn't know anybody and how could I have known about his tooth. I said that didn't matter because God knows you. I told him God knows him from the top of his head to the bottom of his feet. All of a sudden out of nowhere the wet blanket of dead religion appeared. Let's call this religious lady Debbie Downer. She needed healing and in an atmosphere of faith I felt the Holy Spirit touching her. When I asked her if she was healed, she said "No, in fact it is worse!" Immediately the atmosphere had changed from faith to doubt. The spirit of unbelief had arrived. Unbelief isn't a little matter we have to get over but, it is sin. Unbelief has a life of its own and it will rob our blessings.

Unbelief also leads to complacency and entitlement. The Israelites, who had witnessed miracle after miracle—deliverance from Egypt, manna in the wilderness, water from a rock—began to take God's blessings for granted. They stopped noticing His hand, stopped appreciating His provision, and eventually, they started complaining.

Consider the story of a man who lived near Kennedy Space Center. A visitor asked if he ever enjoyed watching the space shuttle launches. "Not anymore," he replied. "I've seen so many launches that I don't even go outside to watch." When I was a new convert, I had seen my first miracle in our church. This evangelist came to our church and had a man sit in a chair. One of his legs seemed at least two inches shorter. The evangelist called over new converts or anyone who wanted to see God do a miracle. When he prayed the other leg shot out and this man had two legs equal size. His back pain instantly left his body. I was blown away. I was so excited because I had never seen anything like that. As I was talking about it the whole afternoon with my soon to be wife Melanie. She confessed something to me. She said "You encourage me." I didn't understand what she meant until she went on and said "I have grown up in church and miracles are just the norm around here." Looking at me she continued. "You see a miracle like this and you are overwhelmed with excitement." "I want to appreciate God's miracles again."

When we stop noticing God's blessings, we quit appreciating them. And when we quit appreciating them, we start complaining.

God's destiny for us requires a heart that values His blessings and sees His hand in every situation.

The difference between Joshua and Caleb and the ten other spies was their faith. While the others saw giants, Joshua and Caleb saw God's promises. While the others doubted, they believed.

In Numbers 14:24, God says of Caleb, "But my servant Caleb, because he has a different spirit and has followed me fully, I will bring into the land into which he went, and his descendants shall possess it." Caleb and Joshua believed that God's plans were for their good, no matter how impossible the circumstances seemed.

Sometimes, believing for blessing requires waiting. Like Tua Tagovailoa, the quarterback who sat on the bench for Alabama until the second half of a championship, we might wonder, "When is my time coming?" But Tua Tagovailoa didn't grow bitter. He stayed faithful, and when the time came, he seized the moment, leading his team to victory in a National Championship.

Similarly, Joshua and Caleb waited decades for their destiny. They endured the consequences of others' unbelief, but their faith remained unshaken. In the end, they stepped into the fullness of God's promise. You know it would of been frustrating to walk past the same mountains, trees, rocks for 40 years. However, God was able to help them remain full of faith and enter into fruitfulness.

Just like the tomatoes in the sinkhole, God's plans for us can thrive even in unlikely circumstances. We may feel stuck, surrounded by difficulties, but God's destiny for us isn't dictated by our environment—it's determined by His purpose.

The question is, will we believe? Will we respond to God's promises with faith, or will we let fear and unbelief rob us of our destiny? It's about allowing God to use us in faith right where we are. My friend Mauricio and I were reading all the books we could find about Smith Wigglesworth, John G Lake and F F Bosworth. One of the books was called "The Apostle of Faith" by Wigglesworth. I had a condition where I couldn't hold food down and there was blood coming out of my throat. I had gone to doctors and they agreed that I would need to have camera go down my esophagus to see where the damage was. As Mauricio and I read about the faith of Wigglesworth for healing we were encouraged. The funny part of this is that Mauricio said God can heal you and he put his hand in a pan of old oil that was used a day ago to cook some eggs and he put his hand on my head. He said forcefully "I command sickness to leave in Jesus's name be healed!" With old oil running down my face I was instantly healed and have never had pain or blood there at all.

God's call to greatness isn't about perfection or the perfect environment—it's about trust. It's about believing that He can use our situation, no matter how messy, to bring about His plans.

So, like Joshua and Caleb, let's have a "different spirit." Let's see the possibilities in God's promises. Let's believe for the blessings He has prepared.

Sometimes faith is standing against the crowd and declaring what God CAN DO. Because in His hands, even a sinkhole can become a garden, and we can step into the greatness for which we were created.

By Joshua L Neal

8. Fulfilled Destiny: Moving Away From The Familiar

There was an old story about a man who used to juggle for his livelihood in a distant country. When he made enough money, he packed his bags and headed for home on a ship. As he waited on this traveling vessel to get him home, because he was drawn to showmanship, he decided to gather a crowd on this ship by his wonderful ability to juggle. The crowds started to gather around and mouths opened wide as they stood in awe. However, his adrenaline for applause he decided to pull out the box where all his money was. After explaining to the crowd that all his livelihood was in this box he began to throw it high in the air. The crowd cheered and yelled "higher!" When he threw it once more the ship jerked and the box with all his money fell overboard. This juggler was broken and left with a big NOW WHAT! The image of a juggler who lost his box is a vivid metaphor for wasted destiny. It is a sobering thought—how many inheritances have been squandered and destinies lost because of poor decisions or fear of stepping into the unknown. Yet, in God's hands, even the most improbable circumstances can lead to a glorious destiny. This truth is powerfully demonstrated in the story of Abram, later known as Abraham, and his journey to fulfill the destiny God had ordained for him.

The world often misrepresents the concept of destiny. In secular culture, destiny is portrayed as self-indulgent—a pursuit of personal fame or fortune. The narrative revolves around showcasing talents, accumulating wealth, or basking in recognition. In this view, destiny is self-made, entirely dependent on human effort and ego. Alternatively, some see destiny as inevitable, something that will unfold regardless of their choices or actions.

In contrast, God's perspective on destiny is profoundly different. Destiny is neither self-serving nor automatic. It is a divine calling that requires intentionality and obedience. Too often, believers fall into misconceptions about destiny. We assume it's reserved for others—those we perceive as more talented, more spiritual, or more gifted. We compare ourselves to others, feeling inadequate and disqualifying ourselves before we even begin. The Apostle Paul cautioned against this kind of thinking:

> ***"But they, measuring themselves by themselves, and comparing themselves among themselves, are not wise"*** -2 Corinthians 10:12

By Joshua L Neal

Another misconception is that destiny has an expiration date. How many times have we heard someone say, "I missed my chance" or "It's too late for me"? Abram's story obliterates this myth. When God called Abram to leave his homeland and pursue his destiny, he was 75 years old. Far from being in the prime of life, Abram was well past the age most would consider ideal for starting anew. Yet his age did not limit God's plans for him. What set Abram apart was not his youth or strength but his willingness to step into God's calling. He understood that God is not held back by boundaries or what would be limitations to us. When we begin to think God is limited we should remind ourselves of what Jesus said:

> ***But Jesus looked at them and said to them, "With men this is impossible, but with God all things are possible."*** -Matthew 19:26 (NKJV)

God's call to Abram in Genesis 12 reveals several important truths about destiny. The first is that destiny often calls us away from what is convenient. Abram was told to leave his country, his family, and his father's house to go to an unknown land. This was no small request. Abram's homeland, Ur, was a thriving cultural and economic hub. It boasted schools, libraries, and significant advancements in mathematics, astronomy, and politics. By all accounts, it was the ideal place to settle and build a life. Yet God called Abram to leave behind the comforts and opportunities of Ur for the uncertainty of a new land.

Destiny also requires us to move away from what is familiar. Leaving his family meant Abram had to step out of the safety net of financial support, emotional encouragement, and shared responsibilities. God's call to destiny is always deeply personal and often contrary to human logic. Many who seek God's will wrestle with this tension. It is not uncommon to find that God's plan is the opposite of what we might choose for ourselves.

One of the greatest challenges in pursuing destiny is the reluctance to take the first step. Many people delay obedience because they want to see the full picture before committing. However, God's ways often unfold one step at a time. Abram's story illustrates this beautifully. God called him to a land He would show him—not a land He had already revealed. Abram had to trust God's character and step out in faith, not knowing the destination. As he obeyed, God's blessings and promises became clearer.

Failure to step into destiny leads to regret and missed opportunities. How many times have we wondered, "What might have been?" when looking back at choices not made? The cost of inaction is not just personal loss but also the loss of God's intended blessings. Genesis 12:2-3 records God's promises to Abram:

> *"I will make you a great nation; I will bless you and make your name great; and you shall be a blessing. I will bless those who bless you, and I will curse him who curses you; and in you all the families of the earth shall be blessed."*

These blessings hinged on Abram's willingness to obey.

Faith and obedience are the keys to unlocking destiny. One pastor shared a humorous yet profound story about a man in his church who tithed down to the penny. Though he started with little, he remained faithful in giving. Over time, God blessed him abundantly, and he became a successful business owner. The principle is clear: obedience, even in small things, opens the door to God's favor.

As Abram walked in obedience, God revealed Himself to him in deeper ways. In Genesis 12:7, the Lord appeared to Abram and reiterated His promise:

> *"To your descendants I will give this land."*

Abram responded by building an altar to the Lord and calling on His name. This act of worship signified Abram's commitment to God and his recognition of God's hand in his destiny.

Abram's actions teach us two critical lessons about fulfilling destiny. First, he pitched his tent, symbolizing his willingness to dwell where God had placed him. He trusted God's promise for the future and made his home in the land of promise, even though it was not yet fully realized. Second, he built an altar, establishing a foundation of worship and dependence on God. The altar was a physical representation of Abram's spiritual commitment.

Walking in destiny is a journey of growth and revelation. As we take steps of obedience, God reveals more of His plan and Himself to us. The progression in Abram's story—from hearing God's call to experiencing His presence—shows that God's ways become clearer as we trust and obey. However, when we resist or delay obedience, we hinder this process. Why would God reveal more if we have not acted on what He has already shown us?

Destiny is not a distant dream or a privilege reserved for a select few. It is God's calling for every believer, a divine purpose designed to bring Him glory and bless others. Like Abram, we must be willing to leave behind what is convenient and familiar, trust God's character, and take the first step in faith. When we do, we position ourselves to experience His promises, grow in our relationship with Him, and fulfill the destiny He has prepared for us. God's plans are always bigger and better than anything we could imagine—but they require our obedience.

Let us, like Abram, respond to God's call with faith and step into the destiny He has designed for us.

9. Destiny & Marriage:
God's Plan For Unity And Purpose

In the book of Genisis God shows us the first marriage. Genesis 1:27-28 "So God created man in his own image, in the image of God he created him; male and female he created them. And God blessed them. And God said to them, 'Be fruitful and multiply and fill the earth and subdue it and have dominion over the fish of the sea and over the birds of the heavens and over every living thing that moves on the earth.'"

Linda Wolfe, a 68-year-old Indiana woman, made headlines for being married 23 times. Her first marriage, at the age of 16, was for love. Subsequent marriages, however, included partners like a one-eyed inmate, two homeless men, and even two husbands who were homosexuals. Over time, each marriage dissolved. Some ended in infidelity, others in abuse, and one even included a husband who padlocked the refrigerator. After 12 years of being single—her longest stint since childhood—Linda reflected on her journey: "I would get married again," she said. "Because, you know, it gets lonely."

What was the root of her endless cycle of marriages? Over time, the excitement wore off, and she realized her partners had flaws. Linda's story offers a mirror to the challenges many couples face—moving from "perfect" to "problematic" when flaws surface.

Genesis introduces us to the first marriage: Adam and Eve. Created by God Himself, they were the literal embodiment of a "match made in heaven." In Eden, everything was perfect—at least initially. God declared His creation "good," including this union. Yet, even in paradise, their relationship faced challenges that echo in marriages today.

In modern times, many singles and spouses are still searching for "the perfect one." Divorce rates reflect this reality, often citing "irreconcilable differences" as the cause. However, at its core, such differences often boil down to selfishness or an unwillingness to adapt. Marriage, as we'll see, requires constant growth and change. It's not about finding perfection but navigating imperfection together.

Consider how some marriages today begin: prenuptial agreements, rigid rules, and expectations for perfection. These agreements outline everything from household chores to weight limits. The message is clear: "If my spouse has flaws, it's over." This mindset leads to fragile relationships, much like the fleeting "drive-thru" weddings and divorces in places like Las Vegas.

The story of Adam and Eve highlights a critical issue in marriage: communication breakdown. After their disobedience, they not only hid from God but also from each other. The intimacy they once shared was replaced with shame, blame, and distrust. Eve acted independently, disregarding both God's command and her husband's role, which fractured their unity. The serpent's strategy wasn't just to sow distrust in God but also to divide their marriage. As Jesus later warned, "A house divided against itself cannot stand."

The fallout was immediate. Adam blamed Eve, and even God, saying, "The woman whom You gave to be with me, she gave me of the tree, and I ate." Adam's accusation reflects how easily we forget the blessings of our spouse and instead focus on their flaws. Yet, God's design for marriage remains: "It is not good for man to be alone."

Adam and Eve's story teaches us that no marriage is perfect. Every couple must face the reality of their flaws and seek a remedy. In the garden, Adam's initial solution was fig leaves—a futile attempt to hide their shortcomings. This mirrors our own tendency to cover up issues rather than address them.

A powerful illustration of this comes from Nathaniel Hawthorne's short story "The Birthmark." A man named Aylmer, obsessed with his wife's beauty, fixated on a small birthmark on her cheek.

By Joshua L Neal

His relentless desire for perfection led to her death. He promised his wife he could remove it but the poor wife bled to death. This serves as a cautionary tale: focusing on how minor flaws can destroy relationships. As the Bible warns, "The little foxes spoil the vine."

Instead of trying to "fix" our spouses, we must recognize our shared humanity. One example is that my wife and I have had some great fights in our relationship. If you say you don't fight in your marriage your relationship is boring. Anyway, Melanie and I had a fight. The problem I have is Melanie has a memory like a computer. She doesn't forget anything. I forget what I did yesterday. When we fight, she will remember details, what I wore, how my face looked, who was there. If I retort and say "I do not believe you!" Out comes the evidence. She will show me pictures, written confessions etc…. You get the point. One wonderful Sunday morning we had a real doozy of a fight and the best news is I won. She was stunted and I was declared king of the mountain. On our way to church she was upset but I was justified because I have had to deal with losses and got over it. I told myself in my head "She always wins and I don't care if she is mad." "She can get over it!" While walking into the church I smiled and shook hands and probably said "God bless you brother!" My Christianize turned on quickly. My wife went to the bathroom and I set our stuff down on her seat and then took my seat. When Melanie came to our seats, I pushed all our stuff out of the way so she could sit down. Instantly God dealt with my heart and said "Just like your making room now for your stuff you need to make room for your wife's flaws." Just like that in an instant even though I won the last battle God said I lost the war. God was teaching me a lesson about marriage. You don't fight to win but you fight to work out flaws in each other to bring you closer together. Jesus' words are instructive: "First, remove the beam from your own eye, and then you can see clearly to remove the speck from your brother's eye." Flawed people cannot perfect each other, but they can work together to grow and strengthen their bond.

Genesis emphasizes that God gave dominion not only to Adam or Eve individually but to both of them as a team: "And God said to them." Marriage thrives on unity. Ecclesiastes 4:9 beautifully illustrates this principle:

> ***"Two are better than one, because they have a good return for their labor. If either of them falls down, one can help the other up."***

In my own marriage, there have been times when I've been weak, and my wife, Melanie, has been strong. Her strength in those moments has been a blessing and a reminder of God's design for partnership.

By Joshua L Neal

> *"He who finds a wife finds a good thing and obtains favor from the Lord."* -Proverbs 18:22

But unity requires effort. Contention in relationships weakens us and displeases God. Malachi 2:14-15 reveals that God is a witness to our marriages, calling us to honor our covenant and treat each other with love and respect.

> *"Above all, love each other deeply, because love covers a multitude of sins"* (1 Peter 4:8).

We can never forget that God designed marriage and He knows how marriage works best. God's blueprint for marriage is found in Genesis 2:24:

> *"A man shall leave his father and mother and be joined to his wife, and they shall become one flesh."*

The word "cleave" signifies unity, adaptation, and assimilation. However, it also has a dual meaning: "to divide." In marriage, we have the choice to either unite or tear apart. God's desire is for us to cleave to one another, creating a bond of love and understanding.

Marriage is not about winning arguments but preserving the relationship. It's about learning your spouse's needs, enjoying each other, and allowing God to guide your union. As Mark 10:9 reminds us:

"What God has joined together, let no one separate."

Adam's actions after the fall are a profound example of redemption. Despite Eve's mistake, Adam named her "Eve," meaning "mother of all living." This act of grace foreshadowed the redemptive power of God's love in marriage. Similarly, our flaws can become opportunities for growth and beauty when God is involved.

I spoke to a guy one time and asked him "Why are you getting married?" I was expecting to hear that they were friends or they enjoyed each other's company. He answered with "I gotta preach bro." Wives were never meant to be just another piece in the puzzle so you can have destiny. She is not meant to be one of marks on your list of requirements for ministry. I didn't marry Melanie because she was one of the trinkets I had to pick up so I can preach God's word. No, we fell in love. In fact, as a newer believer, I had to battle with making her my idol. I loved every moment I spent with her. Her laugh, the way she smiles. If there was a checklist for the right spouse, we would choose wrong every time. Why because we see as man sees. We look on the outward. One young lady in our fellowship was given a checklist by a disciple that read "Can you cook?" Etc.... Instead of focusing on whether or not a future wife needs a checklist why don't you focus on yourself.

By Joshua L Neal

Guys who say "I'm looking for my woman of God." ask first "Am I a man of God?" Or "Am I a woman of God?" Melanie and I were not ready for marriage we were just raw material that God joined together and now He is making and molding us together.

Marriage, like life, is filled with cracks and imperfections. There is an art in Japan called kintsugi. The word kintsugi is Japanese for "gold seams". When a vase breaks, they fill the broken seams with gold. Brokenness is a picture of flaws and gold is a gracious covering of those flaws. Yet, just as gold is used to repair and highlight the beauty of a broken vase, God's presence in our marriages can turn flaws into strength. While we may not be able to change our spouse's internal struggles, we serve a God who can.

When Adam named Eve, he created a path for redemption. If God could help the first couple—even after their sinful fall—He can certainly help us. A marriage with God at its center is like a threefold cord, not easily broken. Invite Him into your marriage union, and watch as He brings healing, restoration, and unity.

10. Fulfilled Destiny: The Overall Picture

When I visited the Prado Museum in Spain, I encountered a unique kind of artwork called "stand back art." Up close, these pieces were confusing, even chaotic. It was only when you stepped back that the full beauty of the painting became clear. Life—and more specifically, our destiny—is much like that. We can't define God's work in our lives based on one bad day, a single decision, or even a challenging season. We have to step back and trust that God is painting a masterpiece that we may not fully comprehend in the moment.

Genesis 49:22–26 offers us a glimpse of this bigger picture, describing the life of Joseph:

> *"Joseph is a fruitful bough, a fruitful bough by a well; his branches run over the wall. The archers have bitterly grieved him, shot at him and hated him. But his bow remained in strength, and the arms of his hands were made strong by the hands of the Mighty God of Jacob... By the Almighty who will bless you with blessings of heaven above, blessings of the deep that lies beneath, blessings of the breasts and of the womb."*

By Joshua L Neal

Joseph's life reminds us that while circumstances may seem disjointed or painful, God's plan is always in motion. Let's explore this truth by stepping back to see the big picture, recognizing God's hand in every stage of our journey, and guarding our hearts to experience His blessings.

Genesis 49 is not just a blessing for Joseph—it's an overview of God's plan at work in a life filled with trials and triumphs. Joseph's story is a model for all believers, revealing that God's purposes unfold over time and often through difficulty.

Joseph's life began with a grand dream: to rule over his family. But the reality he faced seemed to contradict this destiny. Sold into slavery, falsely accused, and imprisoned, Joseph's circumstances could have made him question God's promise. How could someone with such a calling end up as a slave in Egypt?

Many of us ask similar questions: "How can I be fruitful when I'm struggling? How can I fulfill my calling when life seems to be falling apart?" Whether it's a storm that seems insurmountable, a loss that feels unbearable, or a delay that feels eternal, these moments can blur our vision of God's ultimate plan.

Joseph didn't just face difficult circumstances; he also endured the sting of betrayal. The "archers" mentioned in Genesis 49 represent the people who wounded him—his brothers who sold him, the false accusers who lied about him, and others who sought to harm him. People can often be the greatest challenge to our destiny, but Joseph's story reminds us that no human action can thwart God's purposes.

The determining factor in Joseph's life—and in ours—is God. Genesis 49:24 says:

> *"His bow remained in strength, and the arms of his hands were made strong by the hands of the Mighty God of Jacob."*

In every season, God's presence was Joseph's strength, guidance, and stability.

God is described in this passage with several significant names, each revealing an aspect of His character:

The Mighty God of Jacob this means God's power is available to His people, even in their weakness. Joseph's strength didn't come from his circumstances but from God's might.

The Shepherd is quite obvious so we know that God guides His people with care and precision, even when the path seems unclear. Psalm 32:8 echoes this truth:

> *"I will instruct you and teach you in the way you should go; I will counsel you with my eye upon you."*

The Stone of Israel: God is our unshakable foundation, offering stability amidst life's chaos (Isaiah 44:8).

When the Bible says the God of your father this name points to God's covenant faithfulness, showing that His promises endure across generations. God is not a covenant breaker. When He walked through the ravine of blood because of the sacrifices cut in half He puts Abraham asleep and walks alone. Why would God do this since the covenant was let God do this to me as these animals if I break covenant. Well, He put Abraham to sleep because only God could keep that covenant.

God's power has no limits, as Revelation 1:8 reminds us:

> *"I am the Alpha and the Omega... who is and who was and who is to come, the Almighty."*

Joseph's journey teaches us that God is involved in every stage of life—the good, the bad, and the ugly. Even when we don't see it, He is our hidden strength, working behind the scenes to fulfill His purposes.

One of the greatest keys to experiencing God's plan is keeping your heart right. Proverbs 4:23 instructs us:

> ***"Keep your heart with all vigilance, for from it flow the springs of life."***

Trust is essential. If God is truly Almighty and our Shepherd, then we can trust Him even when we don't understand. Job demonstrated this trust when he declared:

> ***"Though he slay me, I will hope in him."*** (Job 13:15).

Trusting God means believing that He is in control, even when others hurt us or circumstances seem unfair.

Joseph also shows us the power of forgiveness. When faced with his brothers—the very ones who sold him into slavery—Joseph told them,

> ***"Do not fear, for am I in the place of God?"*** (Genesis 50:19).

Joesph was saying God has orchestrated events beyond our understanding without finite minds.

A man told a story this way one time. A man was walking along the beach one day and as he walked, he saw a young boy running back and forth from the ocean to a small mound he created with a hole in the middle. When the man asked the boy why he was running back and forth the boy said "I am going to get all that ocean water and put it in my mountain hole." The man laughed and thought this is exactly how we are with God. We think we can fit an infinite God and his plans into our finite minds. It will never work. David gets this revelation one time when he looks at the stars in the heavens and asks God the question "What is man that you are mindful of him?"

You see for Joseph forgiveness isn't about excusing wrongs; it's about releasing others to God and trusting Him to work everything for good.

Finally, Joseph's story highlights the blessings that flow from a life lived in trust and obedience. Genesis 49 describes Joseph as a "fruitful bough by a well" whose branches "run over the wall."

This imagery speaks of supernatural fruitfulness—impact that reaches beyond what we can see. God's blessings extend far beyond our immediate circumstances, touching others and leaving a legacy that lasts.

Just like "stand back art," our lives are best understood from God's perspective. When we focus on the immediate, we may see only confusion, pain, or disappointment. But when we step back and trust God, we begin to see the masterpiece He is creating.

Joseph's life was filled with challenges, but in the end, it was a story of fruitfulness, redemption, and blessing. His journey reminds us that God is always at work, even in the darkest moments. He is the Mighty God of Jacob, the Shepherd who guides us, and the Rock who sustains us.

No matter where you are in life, remember: God's purposes will stand. Keep your heart right, trust in His promises, and stand back to see the masterpiece He is painting.

By Joshua L Neal

11. Crossroads Of Destiny:
How God Shapes Hearts For His Purpose

A famous story about Francis of Assisi. As he felt the call of God on his life, he wrestled with the expectations of his family. Francis held a symbolic funeral with little rocks on the ground in the shape of a wife and some children for his imaginary family—he then proceeded to conduct a funeral for them. It is strange but for him the choice was either family or Destiny and he chose to do what he felt God wanted. Thank God our families can join us in the will of God. Assisi was not trying to dishonor them, but to acknowledge the higher calling God had placed on him. His destiny required a new focus, a new identity, and ultimately, a new heart. This echoes the spiritual transformation we see in Saul's life, as recorded in 1 Samuel 9:27-10:9.

> *As they were going down to the outskirts of the city, Samuel said to Saul, "Tell the servant to go on ahead of us." And he went on. "But you stand here awhile, that I may announce to you the word of God."*
>
> *Then Samuel took a flask of oil and poured it on his head, and kissed him and said: "Is*

it not because the Lord has anointed you commander over His inheritance?

When you have departed from me today, you will find two men by Rachel's tomb in the territory of Benjamin at Zelzah; and they will say to you, 'The donkeys which you went to look for have been found. And now your father has ceased caring about the donkeys and is worrying about you, saying, "What shall I do about my son?"

Then you shall go on forward from there and come to the terebinth tree of Tabor. There three men going up to God at Bethel will meet you, one carrying three young goats, another carrying three loaves of bread, and another carrying a skin of wine.

And they will greet you and give you two loaves of bread, which you shall receive from their hands.

After that you shall come to the hill of God where the Philistine garrison is. And it will happen, when you have come there to the city, that you will meet a group of prophets coming down from the high place with a stringed instrument, a tambourine, a flute, and a harp before them; and they will be prophesying.

By Joshua L Neal

Then the Spirit of the Lord will come upon you, and you will prophesy with them and be turned into another man.

And let it be, when these signs come to you, that you do as the occasion demands; for God is with you.

You shall go down before me to Gilgal; and surely I will come down to you to offer burnt offerings and make sacrifices of peace offerings. Seven days you shall wait, till I come to you and show you what you should do."

So it was, when he had turned his back to go from Samuel, that God gave him another heart; and all those signs came to pass that day.

In the beginning of Saul's story, we find him living a seemingly ordinary life. He was diligently searching for his father's lost donkeys, an errand that seemed mundane and insignificant. Yet, it was in the middle of this routine task that Saul's destiny began to unfold.

It's fascinating to consider how God often calls people in the middle of their everyday lives. Saul's concern for the lost donkeys reveals something crucial about the kind of people God uses—those who are faithful in the small things. Jesus highlighted this principle in the parable of the lost sheep, where the shepherd leaves the ninety-nine to search for the one that is lost. Saul's diligence mirrored this shepherd's heart, even though he didn't yet understand the bigger picture.

Life can often feel like a series of unconnected dots. We go about our daily routines, unaware that God is watching and weaving our lives into His grand design. For Saul, his concern over the donkeys led him to Samuel, the prophet of God, and the crossroads of his destiny.

Picture this moment: Samuel takes a flask of oil, pours it over Saul's head, and anoints him as commander over God's inheritance. This is no ordinary moment. Saul's life—and heart—would never be the same.

As readers, we might marvel at Saul's sudden elevation, but the reality is that God is always searching for those who will embrace His calling. He is looking for individuals who will stand in the gap, as Isaiah once described. Saul's moment of anointing was both a privilege and a test—one that all great men and women of God must face. Will we surrender to God's will, even when it takes us out of our comfort zones? Will we, like Jesus, say, "Not my will, but Yours be done"?

By Joshua L Neal

As Samuel gave Saul detailed instructions about the journey ahead, something extraordinary happened. Verse 9 tells us, "So it was, when he had turned his back to go from Samuel, that God gave him another heart; and all those signs came to pass that day."

This is a powerful truth: the fulfillment of destiny requires a new heart. A heart touched by God. A heart that is willing and obedient. Think of Peter, who stepped out of the boat at Jesus 'command. Or Paul, who declared, "I am ready to be poured out like a drink offering." Their willingness to follow God's call was rooted in hearts transformed by His power.

The Bible teaches that we have the ability to set our hearts, for good or for evil. Ecclesiastes 8:11 warns that the heart of man can become fully set on evil when consequences are delayed. Before salvation, many of us pursued sin with determination, setting our hearts on fulfilling selfish desires. But when God gives us a new heart, everything changes. We begin to desire what is right and pleasing to Him.

Helen Good Brenneman once wrote about the need for kindness and the incompatibility of a mean spirit with a kind heart. She described a man who underwent a literal heart transplant, but his body rejected the kind heart because he was a mean-spirited man. Similarly, without surrendering to God, our hearts cannot align with His will. The good news is that we can set our hearts to seek the Lord, as 2 Chronicles 11:16 describes. When Saul walked away from Samuel, he didn't just leave with a new title; he left with a new heart.

A new heart is not something we can manufacture on our own. It is a supernatural work of God. As Ezekiel 11:19 promises, "Then I will give them one heart, and I will put a new spirit within them, and take the stony heart out of their flesh, and give them a heart of flesh."

God is the ultimate heart surgeon, replacing hearts of stone with hearts of flesh. He doesn't just improve us; He transforms us. This transformation is both an invitation and a command. Ezekiel 18:31 urges:

> ***"Cast away from you all the transgressions which you have committed, and get yourselves a new heart and a new spirit."***

This new heart gives us the capacity to walk in God's statutes and fulfill His purposes, as Ezekiel 36:26-27 declares.

For Saul, the transformation began with a meeting with God. That same opportunity is available to us. When we surrender to God, whether in salvation or in the pursuit of our calling, He gives us a new heart. It is through this new heart that we find the strength, desire, and courage to walk into our destiny.

The story of Francis of Assisi's symbolic funeral reminds us that answering God's call often requires letting go of old attachments. Like Saul, we must turn our backs on the past and walk forward with the new heart God gives us. Whether we are searching for lost donkeys or navigating the crossroads of our destiny, God is ready to meet us, anoint us, and transform us.

The question is: Will we surrender? Will we allow Him to give us a new heart for the journey ahead? The answer to these questions determines not just the course of our lives but the impact we will have for eternity.

12. Destiny Alliances:
Strong And Wrong Alliances

The alliances we form have the power to shape our lives and determine our destinies. In 2 Kings 3:1–7, we encounter a story of alliances—both strong and wrong. This passage introduces King Jehoram of Israel and King Jehoshaphat of Judah. Jehoram, though less wicked than his parents, continued in the sins of his forefathers, while Jehoshaphat sought to walk in righteousness before God. When Jehoram invited Jehoshaphat to join him in battle against Moab, Jehoshaphat agreed without seeking God's guidance. This alliance offers profound lessons about the impact of aligning ourselves with the wrong people.

Life is not meant to be lived alone. The Bible teaches us that strength is found in unity:

> *"Though one may be overpowered by another, two can withstand him. And a threefold cord is not quickly broken"* - Ecclesiastes 4:12).

Even from the beginning, God declared:

> *"It is not good that man should be alone"* (Genesis 2:18).

This truth underscores our need for relationships in every area of life: friendships, marriages, business partnerships, and even battles. However, not all alliances are beneficial. Jehoram's invitation to Jehoshaphat highlights the danger of assuming that all partnerships are God-ordained.

Jehoram inherited the throne of Israel and the sins of his lineage. His father, Jeroboam, had reintroduced idolatry by making golden calves (1 Kings 12:28). This act mirrored Aaron's sin in the wilderness, showing how demonic influences can persist through generations. Jehoram's lack of spiritual integrity set the stage for an alliance that would test Jehoshaphat's discernment. In other words, he was functioning on a faulty foundation.

Jehoshaphat, a righteous king, walked in the ways of his father Asa and sought to please God. However, his journey reveals a common struggle among believers: loneliness and the pressure to compromise. Proverbs 18:1 warns, "A man who isolates himself seeks his own desire; he rages against all wise judgment." In his desire for unity, Jehoshaphat agreed to align with Jehoram, assuming that their shared heritage as Israelites justified the partnership. This assumption led to a hasty and unwise decision. He would be making a wrong decision about who he is calling his alliance.

When we align ourselves with others without seeking God's direction, we risk walking in circles and ending up in dry places—both spiritually and practically.

Jehoram and Jehoshaphat's journey to battle against Moab revealed the cracks in their partnership:

> *"Then he said, 'Which way shall we go up?' And he answered, 'By way of the Wilderness of Edom.' So the king of Israel went with the king of Judah and the king of Edom, and they marched on that roundabout route seven days; and there was no water for the army, nor for the animals that followed them"* (2 Kings 3:8–9).

When God is not consulted, even strong alliances falter. Their reliance on human wisdom led to frustration and lack. The same applies to our relationships—whether in marriage, friendships, or business. If God's guidance is absent, the partnership becomes a source of dryness rather than refreshment.

> **"Let them alone. They are blind leaders of the blind. And if the blind leads the blind, both will fall into a ditch"** (Matthew 15:14).

Jehoram's alliance with Jehoshaphat highlights another key issue: misplaced trust. Jeremiah 17:5–6 warns:

By Joshua L Neal

> *"Cursed is the man who trusts in man and makes flesh his strength, whose heart departs from the Lord. For he shall be like a shrub in the desert, and shall not see when good comes."*

Many people stay in wrong alliances out of misplaced hope, believing things will improve. Whether it's a toxic relationship or an unhealthy business deal, the longer we remain in these alliances, the more we suffer spiritually and emotionally. There is a psychological disorder that is called Solomon's Paradox. I am not a psychologist but in my own words it is based off of Solomon in the Bible. Solomon writes about staying away from the seductive woman and then he has many wives in concubines who served foreign gods. So, the obvious question is why are you not taking your own advice Solomon. People do this all the time. They have great advised for other people but they won't apply that same wisdom to their own lives. In this story poor choices are made without consulting God.

The good news is that God's grace is available, even when we've made poor choices. Jehoshaphat eventually sought the counsel of a prophet:

> *"But Jehoshaphat said, 'Is there no prophet of the Lord here, that we may inquire of the Lord by him?' So one of the servants of the king of Israel answered and said, 'Elisha the*

> *son of Shaphat is here, who poured water on the hands of Elijah'"* (2 Kings 3:11).

Elisha's response was firm:

> *"As the Lord of hosts lives, before whom I stand, surely were it not that I regard the presence of Jehoshaphat king of Judah, I would not look at you, nor see you"* (2 Kings 3:14).

Despite his disgust at the alliance, Elisha sought God's direction. His instructions were unexpected:

> *"Make this valley full of ditches. For thus says the Lord: 'You shall not see wind, nor shall you see rain; yet that valley shall be filled with water, so that you, your cattle, and your animals may drink'"* (2 Kings 3:16–17).

God's miraculous provision reminds us that He can redeem our mistakes and provide a way forward, even in the wilderness of bad decisions.

Elisha's example teaches us to seek divine direction before moving forward. God's plans often defy human logic, but they lead to provision and victory. Just as the kings needed to dig ditches in preparation for God's miracle, we must actively trust and obey His instructions. When I was a new convert, I was struggling and an usher made a comment to someone else. He told another brother in the church "Just because the mouse is in the cookie jar, It doesn't mean the mouse is a cookie." Words meant for someone else brought me wisdom.

Strong alliances can propel us toward our God-given destiny, but wrong alliances can derail us. Jehoshaphat's story serves as both a cautionary tale and a reminder of God's grace. When we find ourselves in dry places due to poor decisions, it's never too late to turn back to God. By seeking His guidance and aligning ourselves with His will, we can experience the refreshing waters of His provision and walk confidently into our destiny.

13. Destiny In The Middle Of His Will: Finding Purpose Through Life's Troubles

God wants us in the Middle of His Will. I had an art teacher who yelled at me because while trying to make a vase on a potter's wheel I was goofing around. With my clay I was trying to spin the wheel so fast clay would go everywhere. When she yelled, she said "Keep the clay in the middle of the wheel!" This really applies to our chapter. We like the clay that we are must stay in the middle of God's will.

Psalm 138:7-8 (NKJV) says:

> *Though I walk in the midst of trouble, You will revive me; You will stretch out Your hand Against the wrath of my enemies, And Your right hand will save me. The Lord will perfect that which concerns me; Your mercy, O Lord, endures forever; Do not forsake the works of Your hands.*

Life's troubles are an undeniable reality. The psalmist captures this truth: often, we find ourselves walking right through the middle of difficult and trying situations. Troubles come in many forms—

whether external challenges or internal battles of fear, anxiety, and doubt. Like David, we often need revival amid relentless trouble.

No one enjoys trouble. If we had the option to make progress in life without difficulty, we'd gladly choose that path. Trouble wears on us, as Paul describes in 2 Corinthians 7:5:

> *"For indeed, when we came to Macedonia, our bodies had no rest, but we were troubled on every side. Outside were conflicts, inside were fears."*

Trouble is exhausting, whether it's external pressures or internal fears that plague us. It's natural to want to avoid trouble, but avoiding it entirely is impossible.

David's cry in Psalm 138:7 acknowledges his need for God's reviving power. His enemies—both human and spiritual—were relentless. Spiritual battles often involve inward struggles such as condemnation, anxiety, and lies that can cloud our thoughts. As 2 Corinthians 10:4-5 reminds us:

> *"The weapons of our warfare are not carnal but mighty in God for pulling down strongholds… bringing every thought into captivity to the obedience of Christ."*

Even David's famous words in Psalm 23:4: "Yea, though I walk through the valley of the shadow of death, I will fear no evil," reflect his experience with fear and difficulty. At times, our troubles may even be self-inflicted. Yet, no matter the source, God's presence and guidance are essential.

An illustration from a pottery class can help us understand the importance of staying in the middle of God's will. A teacher once instructed her students to keep the clay centered on the wheel. When the clay veered off-center, it became impossible to mold. Similarly, our lives are most stable and purposeful when we remain in the middle of God's will.

Being in God's will doesn't mean the absence of trouble, but it brings peace amidst the chaos. The Hebrew text of Psalm 138:7 can be understood to mean, "Go on in the center of trouble." When we're aligned with God's purposes, we can find peace even in the storm.

The story of the prodigal son illustrates this truth. While in his father's house, the son had security, identity, and provision. The moment he stepped outside his father's will, his life spiraled into chaos. Jonah's story also shows the consequences of leaving God's will. When Jonah fled to Tarshish instead of heading to Nineveh, he faced a terrifying storm and was swallowed by a great fish. Yet, God's mercy brought him back to fulfill His purpose.

Many things can tempt us to walk outside of God's will, such as unhealthy relationships or a desire for control. Amos 3:3 asks, "Can two walk together, unless they are agreed?" Satan's strategies to tempt Jesus in the wilderness offer insight into common pitfalls:

Physical temptation:

"Do what feels right." (Matthew 4:3-4)

Emotional temptation:

"Question God's love." (Matthew 4:5-7)

Control temptation:

"Take over and do it your way." (Matthew 4:8-10)

Even well-meaning people can unintentionally pull us away from God's will. Jesus' own family tried to distract Him from His mission (Matthew 12:46-50), but He stayed focused on His Father's work.

Outside of God's will, confusion and doubt creep in. We may ask, "Why is God's will for my life so hard?" Yet, His will is where we find true peace, even in difficulty.

David's prayer in Psalm 138:8 is a declaration of trust: "The Lord will perfect that which concerns me." God is deeply committed to the work He is doing in our lives. He promised Joshua, "I will never leave you nor forsake you" (Joshua 1:5), and this promise holds true for us.

The prophet Habakkuk also prayed for God's intervention during trying times:

> ***"O Lord, revive Your work in the midst of the years! In wrath remember mercy"*** (Habakkuk 3:2).

When life's troubles seem unending, we can trust that God is still working. Whether we're dealing with aging, illness, or prolonged challenges, His right hand will strengthen and guide us.

Consider the story of a little boy who was attacked by an alligator while playing in a pond. His father saw the danger, ran to his rescue, and grabbed the boy's arms as the alligator clamped down on his legs. In a fierce tug-of-war, the father's grip won, saving his son's life. Later, when asked about his scars, the boy proudly said, "These are from my father refusing to let me go."

God's commitment to us is just as fierce. He refuses to let go, no matter how dire our situation seems. Romans 8:28 assures us that "All things work together for good to those who love God, to those who are the called according to His purpose." And 1 Corinthians 2:9 reminds us that God has unimaginable blessings prepared for those who love Him.

By Joshua L Neal

When we remain in the middle of His will, we can trust that He will perfect His work in us. He will renew our strength, as Isaiah 40:31 promises:

> *"Those who wait on the Lord shall renew their strength; they shall mount up with wings like eagles, they shall run and not be weary, they shall walk and not faint."*

Stay in the center of His will, for it is there that His right hand will sustain, guide, and revive you.

14. Evangelistic Destiny:
Empowered To Reach The World

Evangelism is our destiny. It is woven into the fabric of the Kingdom of God, and there is no calling or purpose within His Kingdom that does not ultimately align with sharing the good news. The heartbeat of God is for lost souls—a love so deep and relentless that He sent His only Son to die for the world (John 3:16). If we are truly followers of Christ, His heart for the lost will become our heartbeat as well.

Acts 1:4-11 provides a powerful picture of how Jesus prepared His disciples for their evangelistic destiny. These verses are not just historical; they are deeply instructive and empowering for believers today. G Cambell Morgan said that the book in the Bible is called acts because the disciples acted. In other words, they put feet to their faith and the good news was that people can be forgiven and set free. The good news that we can know God and have a relationship with Him. Paul said "That I may know him."

Let's explore what this passage reveals about our calling, the equipping we need, and the distractions we must overcome to fulfill our destiny.

Before His ascension, Jesus gave His disciples a vital command:

> ***"Do not depart from Jerusalem, but wait for the Promise of the Father"*** -Acts 1:4

This was a moment of preparation. The disciples were about to embark on the greatest mission ever given to mankind—to bring the gospel to the ends of the earth. But first, they needed to be equipped. Jesus emphasized the necessity of the Holy Spirit, telling them,

> ***"You shall receive power when the Holy Spirit has come upon you; and you shall be witnesses to Me in Jerusalem, and in all Judea and Samaria, and to the end of the earth"*** -Acts 1:8

This principle is still true today. We cannot accomplish God's work in our own strength. The Holy Spirit is the power source for evangelism. It is He who convicts the world of sin (John 16:8), brings clarity to the gospel message, and enables us to overcome fear and hesitation. Without the Spirit, we are unequipped for the vast task before us. As Jesus said, the harvest is plentiful, but the laborers are few (Luke 10:2). How can we labor effectively without His power?

CT Studd, a missionary to China and Africa, famously said, "Some wish to live within the sound of a church or chapel bell; I want to run a rescue shop within a yard of hell." This is the boldness and urgency we need—and it comes from the Holy Spirit's equipping. When we are filled with His power, we are sensitive to His voice and ready to act. Stories abound of believers who were prompted by the Spirit to share the gospel at just the right moment, leading to life-changing encounters.

Despite the clear command to evangelize, many believers struggle to stay focused on this mission. Distractions abound in our modern world: politics, social media, personal comforts, and even our families can pull us away from God's priorities. In Acts 1:6, the disciples themselves were distracted, asking Jesus, "Lord, will You at this time restore the kingdom to Israel?" They were more concerned with political restoration than spiritual transformation. Jesus redirected their focus, saying, "It is not for you to know times or seasons which the Father has put in His own authority. But you shall receive power when the Holy Spirit has come upon you; and you shall be witnesses to Me…" (Acts 1:7-8).

Like the disciples, we can become preoccupied with our own agendas. Some Christians create excuses for not evangelizing, saying, "It's not my gift," or, "Someone else will do it." Others are paralyzed by fear, laziness, or apathy. But Jesus' words in Acts 1:8 leave no room for passivity: "You shall be witnesses." This is not a suggestion; it is a command.

Imagine a soccer goalie distracted by butterflies in the middle of a game, letting the ball roll past him. This is how we appear when we lose sight of our evangelistic purpose. It's not that we are doing evil things; we're just not focused on what matters most. Jesus calls us to refocus, to lift our eyes from the temporary concerns of this world and fix them on the eternal. Sometimes apathy has set in and we just don't care about the lost. One old quote said it this way "Some saints are asleep at the foot of the cross."

The truth is that we must be Refocused, Refueled, and Ready for evangelism.

Acts 1:4-11 is not just about preparation; it's about refocusing and empowering the disciples for the mission ahead. Jesus redirected their attention to what truly mattered and promised the Holy Spirit to refuel their passion and courage. This same process is essential for us today. We need to refocus on the eternal significance of evangelism, refuel through prayer and the Holy Spirit, and step out ready to fulfill our calling.

When the Holy Spirit empowers us, evangelism becomes less about our abilities and more about God's.

We are His ambassadors, carrying the message of reconciliation to a lost world -2 Corinthians 5:18-20

This is not just about building the biggest church or achieving personal recognition; it is about rescuing souls from the clutches of sin and bringing them into the family of God.

Consider this: someone once shared the gospel with you. Perhaps they were nervous or unsure of how you would respond, but they obeyed the Spirit's prompting. Because of their obedience, your life was forever changed. Now it is your turn to carry that message forward. The harvest is great, and the laborers are still few.

Will you step into your evangelistic destiny? Or will you run like Jonah. Jonah decides to run to Tarshish modern day Spain. Now whether his personal dream was to go there so that it was the quickest ship to get away from God's promptings to save souls from peril. He ran. We have to ask ourselves the question of "Why do we run from personal evangelism?" If I am honest there are times where I can justify that I do enough preaching and teaching in my own church with three sermons and one Sunday school in a week. However, God wants to be able to use our lives to save the lost at all times.

By Joshua L Neal

Evangelism is not just a task; it is the very heartbeat of God. Jesus' final command to His disciples before His ascension was to be His witnesses to the ends of the earth (Acts 1:8).

This command echoes throughout history, calling each generation of believers to rise and take their place in the mission field. The world is vast, and the need is urgent. But we are not alone. The Holy Spirit equips us, refuels us, and goes before us, ensuring that we are never laboring in vain.

As Jesus ascended into heaven, two angels appeared, asking the disciples:

"Why do you stand gazing up into heaven?" (Acts 1:11).

This question challenges us today. Are we standing idly by, distracted or hesitant, while the world desperately needs the hope we carry? Or are we stepping forward, empowered by the Spirit, to fulfill our evangelistic destiny?

The time is now. Refocus. Refuel. Get ready. And go. The harvest awaits.

15. Destiny Dominion: Re-Establishing Dominion

When we come to Christ, God establishes dominion in our lives. Old chains are broken, new freedom is found, and His authority begins to shape every part of who we are. But dominion isn't automatic—it must be actively maintained and continually reinforced. If we become idle or neglect the spiritual ground we've been given, the enemy will find a way to disrupt it. In this chapter, we'll explore the life of Isaac in Genesis 26 and discover how to re-establish dominion when the enemy has tried to take what's rightfully ours.

Time has a way of eroding even the most important things if they're not nurtured. Isaac's story begins with a powerful truth: the Philistines had stopped up the wells of his father, Abraham. These wells, once a source of life and refreshment, had been rendered useless over a period of time.

> *"And Isaac dug again the wells of water which they had dug in the days of Abraham his father, for the Philistines had stopped them up after the death of Abraham."* - Genesis 26:18

This paints a vivid picture of what happens when dominion is left unattended. Wells are symbolic of the blessings, authority, and spiritual freedom God gives us. When we fail to maintain what God has established, the enemy comes to block, disrupt, and steal what was once ours.

Isaac's first step was to go back to the old wells and dig them again. Why? Because dominion often has an expiration date when left unguarded. Many Christians experience this—they once walked in freedom, peace, and spiritual authority, but over time, they allowed distractions, temptations, or complacency to take over.

Isaac's story reminds us that dominion isn't automatic, and the enemy doesn't relinquish ground without a fight. When Isaac's servants dug in the valley and found a well of running water, the herdsmen of Gerar quarreled with them, claiming, "The water is ours!" Isaac named the well Esek, meaning "quarrel." When they dug another well, the same thing happened. He named it Sitnah, meaning "enmity."

This shows us that the enemy always fights to reclaim ground when we try to re-establish dominion. It's a spiritual principle seen throughout Scripture. Samson, for example, assumed his strength and authority didn't require ongoing righteousness. But when he neglected his spiritual commitment, he lost his strength.

> *"And she said, 'The Philistines are upon you, Samson' So he awoke from his sleep and said, 'I will go out as before, at other times, and shake myself free! 'But he did not know that the Lord had departed from him."*
> -Judges 16:20

One of enemy's strategy is to take what God has given you. The wells Isaac reopened were not just sources of water—they were symbols of blessing, refreshment, and life for his family and future generations. Isaac understood this deeply. These wells were a reminder of the dominion and freedom his father Abraham had experienced. Similarly, the dominion God establishes in our lives is meant to bless us, our families, and those around us. It includes spiritual authority, freedom from sin, peace of mind, and fruitfulness in our relationships and ministries.

But the enemy works tirelessly to disrupt these areas. He creates conflict, temptation, and distractions to make it seem easier to abandon the fight rather than re-dig the wells. For some, the enemy uses outright sin. For others, it's more subtle—like complacency, laziness, or distractions such as social media, politics, or personal agendas.

The key to maintaining dominion is to evaluate the condition of your heart regularly. As Lamentations 3:40-41 reminds us:

"Let us search out and examine our ways, and turn back to the Lord; Let us lift our hearts and hands to God in heaven."

Isaac's decision to confront the Philistines by naming the wells "Esek" (quarrel) and "Sitnah" (enmity) teaches us the importance of addressing the enemy directly. Whether the battle is external—like temptation—or internal, such as our own disobedience, we must face it head-on.

Isaac's perseverance paid off. After moving on from Esek and Sitnah, he dug another well and found peace. There was no more quarreling, and he named the well Rehoboth, meaning "spaciousness" or "room." He declared, "For now the Lord has made room for us, and we shall be fruitful in the land."

This is God's heart for us. He desires to make room for us—to bless us and cause us to flourish. But for that to happen, we must be willing to confront the enemy and move forward in faith. We can't allow old habits, distractions, or opposition to keep us from the fullness of God's plan.

Isaac's journey didn't end with Rehoboth. That same night, God appeared to him with a powerful promise:

> ***"I am the God of your father Abraham; do not fear, for I am with you. I will bless you and multiply your descendants for My servant Abraham's sake."*** -Genesis 26:24

This moment represents the culmination of re-establishing dominion. God shows us in a number of ways one way is God visits us and meets us where we are. God also reminds that He will reaffirm His promises and His faithfulness. With Isaac God repeats the blessing: He reassures us of His unchanging covenant. The exciting truth is that God undergirds. He strengthens us for the road ahead.

Isaac responded by building an altar and worshiping God. He pitched his tent and made the decision to dwell in God's promise.

Re-establishing dominion is not always easy, but it is necessary. Like Isaac, we must return to the wells God has given us, dig again, and refuse to let the enemy keep what belongs to us. Whether it's spiritual freedom, peace, ministry, or relationships, God has more for us—but we must fight for it.

Take heart in this: God's desire is to make room for you. He wants you to be fruitful, blessed, and flourishing. But it starts with a decision to re-establish the dominion He's given you and maintain it with diligence. When I got saved, I used to pray on this old chair in the house. It was my altar. What I mean by this is that I learned pretty early that God asks some hard things sometimes. The reason why these are hard is because we like them. We have strong wills at time. So, I told God that I would come to this chair and bend my will to His anytime I disagreed. It really helped because half the time I didn't know why God wanted this or that decision made.

However, time really is a revealer of God's purposes. Every time I agreed and waited for stuff to play out God was and is always right. I said that to say this, dominion is all about surrendering to what God wants. So, dig deep. Refuse to let the enemy keep what God has given you. And remember, the God is with you—just as He was with Isaac. The wells are waiting; it's time to re-establish dominion.

16. Guarding Destiny:
Protecting the treasure within

Every treasure chest holds its value not because of the box itself but because of what's inside. No one admires an empty container, no matter how ornate. Similarly, our hearts—representing our inner selves, thoughts, desires, and will—are the real treasure. What's inside our hearts defines our identity, shapes our decisions, and ultimately directs our lives.

Proverbs 4:23 reminds us of the importance of guarding our hearts:

> ***"Keep your heart with all diligence, for out of it spring the issues of life."***

What's inside your heart today? Are you guarding it, or have you left it vulnerable to influences that lead you away from God? Let's dive into the reality of the heart, the dangers of neglecting it, and how God's grace equips us to protect this treasure.

The Bible speaks frequently about the heart—not as a physical organ but as the seat of our identity. Proverbs 23:7 says, "As he thinks in his heart, so is he." What you carry in your heart becomes who you are. It influences your speech, your actions, and your relationships. Jesus Himself said in Luke 6:45:

> *"A good man out of the good treasure of his heart brings forth good; and an evil man out of the evil treasure of his heart brings forth evil. For out of the abundance of the heart his mouth speaks."*

This means the condition of your heart determines the quality of your life. If you hold onto good treasure—faith, love, humility, and truth—your life will reflect those virtues. But if your heart becomes filled with bitterness, sin, or deceit, it will corrupt every part of your life.

In our walk with God, guarding our hearts is not optional; it's vital. The Bible warns us to keep our hearts diligently. The word "keep" implies effort, vigilance, and intentionality. Why? Because the enemy of our souls seeks to corrupt our hearts by introducing influences that God disapproves of—temptations, lies, and distractions.

An unchecked heart is a vulnerable heart. Left unattended, it can become a breeding ground for sin, just as a neglected field grows weeds. In Psalm 51:10, David cries out after his fall into sin, "Create in me a clean heart, O God, and renew a steadfast spirit within me." He understood that sin left unchecked can rot the heart, just as decaying carcasses during ancient sieges poisoned entire cities.

Solomon's words in Proverbs 4 offer wisdom for guarding our hearts by addressing three key areas:

What You Say, "Put away from you a deceitful mouth, and put perverse lips far from you." (Proverbs 4:24) Jesus taught that our words are a direct reflection of what's in our hearts. Gossip, lies, and negativity don't just hurt others—they reveal a deeper issue within us. Guarding our speech is a vital part of protecting our hearts.

What You See, "Let your eyes look straight ahead, and your eyelids look right before you." (Proverbs 4:25) What we allow into our hearts through our eyes can shape our thoughts and desires. Job understood this when he made a covenant with his eyes not to look lustfully at a woman (Job 31:1). Beyond purity, distractions and temptations often appear in our peripheral vision, tempting us to stray from God's path.

"Ponder the path of your feet, and let all your ways be established." (Proverbs 4:26)

Our choices determine the direction of our lives. An established path is one that is deliberate and purposeful, knowing where it leads. Wandering into places—physically or spiritually—that tempt or ensnare us is a recipe for disaster.

In verse 27, Solomon sums it up perfectly:

"Do not turn to the right or the left; remove your foot from evil."

Keeping our hearts involves both avoiding the wrong influences and actively choosing the right ones.

Guarding your heart isn't just about removing bad influences; it's also about filling it with good things. The Word of God is one of the greatest treasures we can store in our hearts.

Psalm 119:11 says, *"Your word I have hidden in my heart, that I might not sin against You."*

When God's Word is in our hearts, we are equipped to resist temptation and handle life's challenges with wisdom and grace. Similarly, prayer is a powerful tool for guarding our hearts. Philippians 4:6-7 encourages us:

"Be anxious for nothing, but in everything by prayer and supplication, with thanksgiving, let your requests be made known to God; and the peace of God, which surpasses all understanding, will guard your hearts and minds through Christ Jesus."

Another critical aspect of guarding our hearts is setting boundaries.

Psalm 101:3-4 provides a practical guide:

"I will set nothing wicked before my eyes; I hate the work of those who fall away; it shall not cling to me. A perverse heart shall depart from me; I will not know wickedness."

Boundaries protect us from influences that could harm our relationship with God. This might mean being mindful of what we watch, read, or listen to, as well as the company we keep.

Guarding your heart is not something you can do alone. We must rely on God's grace to help us overcome. This begins with asking honest questions: "Does this bring me closer to God or further from Him?" Prayer becomes strategic when we invite God to help us guard our hearts.

Behind our church in Blythe California there was a vine that came out of the ground and it would stop the gate from opening. Me and four other disciples in the church had taken a whack at destroying this weed. I think the list of our weaponry included fire, poison, brute strength, and blunt trauma with a pick axe. No matter what we did this green enemy returned. The problem was what was under the surface. The root was what needed to go. This is true of our hearts we must allow the Holy Spirit to reveal the root.

When we face struggles, His grace empowers us to stay the course. 2 Corinthians 12:9 reminds us:

"My grace is sufficient for you, for My strength is made perfect in weakness."

God's grace doesn't just help us identify areas of weakness; it strengthens us to address them. Through His Spirit, we can develop hearts that reflect His love, truth, and righteousness.

A guarded heart is a thriving heart. What we allow inside determines the direction of our lives, the depth of our faith, and the fruitfulness of our walk with God.

Proverbs 4:23 challenges us to guard our hearts with diligence because "out of it spring the issues of life." So let us protect this treasure by watching what we say, where we look, and where we go. Let us fill our hearts with God's Word, surround ourselves with godly influences, and lean on His grace daily.

Remember, your heart is the wellspring of your life. Guard it, nurture it, and fill it with the treasure of God's truth. It's worth the effort, because a guarded heart leads to a life that glorifies Him.

17. Destined To Stand In The Gap: Answering God's Call

Throughout history, there have been moments of great urgency when the need for a man to rise up and take a stand has been undeniable. Some of those men became heroes, their stories etched into history books and passed down for generations. Others remain unsung, but their actions were no less crucial.

The Bible recounts one such moment in Ezekiel 22:30:

> *"So I sought for a man among them who would make a wall, and stand in the gap before Me on behalf of the land, that I should not destroy it; but I found no one."*

This verse is both inspiring and heartbreaking. God was searching for a man—just one man—to intercede for a broken nation, to stand in the gap and protect the land from judgment. Yet He found none. Today, God is still searching. The question is, will He find you?

There have always been moments in history when men were desperately needed. Consider Paul Revere during the American Revolution, risking his life to warn others of an impending attack. He didn't hesitate, knowing that lives depended on his courage and action.

The same is true in the Bible. God has always recognized and used men willing to step into the gap. Men like Noah, who stood out in an ungodly generation; Job, who remained faithful in trials; Jeremiah, who carried God's message even when no one listened; and Isaiah, who boldly answered God's call, saying, "Here am I! Send me."

These men weren't perfect. Some, like Jeremiah, didn't see the results they hoped for. But they stood in the gap, and God counted them as faithful. The lesson is clear: God doesn't need perfection—He needs obedience.

Yet today, many men have forgotten the urgency of God's will. We work tirelessly for earthly rewards but struggle to give God even ten minutes of our time. The Bible reminds us in 2 Corinthians 10:4 that "the weapons of our warfare are not carnal but mighty in God for pulling down strongholds." This is spiritual work, and it has eternal significance.

When God calls, it's not a casual invitation—it's a divine mandate. He's looking for men who will step into the gap and fight for their families, their churches, and their generation.

But where are the men? That's the haunting question of our time. In Ezekiel's day, the people of Jerusalem had become comfortable and complacent. They were entangled in sin—treating parents with contempt, exploiting foreigners, oppressing widows and orphans, and profaning what was holy. They slandered, worshiped idols, took bribes, and lived in rampant sexual immorality.

The sins were many, but the absence of godly men made it worse. As Proverbs 20:6 says:

"Most men will proclaim each his own goodness, but who can find a faithful man?"

Today, the situation is eerily similar. Many men are struggling, not because they lack potential but because they've allowed distractions, sin, and apathy to take root in their hearts. Here are several examples:

Hidden Sin: Secret struggles that drain spiritual strength.

Entertainment Mentality: A life consumed by leisure and self-gratification. Scrolling social media and being consumed by it.

Reversed Roles: Allowing others to take the lead when God has called men to lead.

Pride and Laziness: Refusing to do the small tasks that build character and faith.

Backslidden Hearts: Apathy toward the house of God and the work of ministry. Ezekiel 22:30 asks, "So I sought for a man among them…" The saddest part of this verse isn't that judgment was near; it's that God couldn't find anyone to stand in the gap. Imagine the heartbreak of a God ready to redeem, only to find no one willing to partner with Him.

So, the question remains: Where are the men? More importantly, where are you?

God's heart has always been for redemption. He is merciful, longing to save and restore. But His plan for redemption often involves men who are willing to stand in the gap.

When men fail to rise, the cost is staggering. Churches grow cold, families fall apart, and entire generations drift further from God. Yet when men step up, the ripple effects are transformative.

A redemptive heart is one that aligns with God's heart. It's a heart that sees the urgency of the hour and refuses to sit on the sidelines. It's a heart that says, "I can't be comfortable missing church or neglecting ministry because God has called me to something greater."

God isn't looking for perfection. He's not interested in "momma's boys" or men who play games with their faith. He's looking for men who will: Prioritize His kingdom over their own comfort. These are those who are willing to put their dreams and aspirations aside for the Kingdom of God. Sometimes this means their careers or personal goals. It is asking God what He wants.

As men we are called to lead our families in righteousness.

Serve faithfully, even in the small things. My first ministry was cleaning bathrooms in our church. I wish I could say that I was singing "Jesus is alive while I served wholeheartedly but the truth was that I hated it. This was until I read where the Bible said:

> ***And whatever you do, do it heartily, as to the Lord and not to men, knowing that from the Lord you will receive the reward of the inheritance; for you serve the Lord Christ.*** - Colossians 3:23–24

Stand boldly against sin, both in their own lives and in the world around them.

Ephesians 6:6-7 reminds us to serve not as men-pleasers but as bondservants of Christ, doing His will from the heart. True service to God is driven by a passion for His glory, not the applause of others.

God is still searching. He's looking for men who will build walls of protection around their families, their churches, and their communities. He's looking for men who will stand in the gap and intercede for a broken and lost generation.

The question is, will He find you? Will you rise to the occasion, or will you let apathy and distraction hold you back?

This is the final challenge: Be the man God is searching for. Let your life be a testimony of faith, courage, and obedience. Stand in the gap and make a difference that echoes into eternity.

The time is now. God's redemption is at the door, and He's waiting for a man to answer the call. Will that man be you?

ALTAR CALL

WHETHER YOU READ THIS BOOK OR STUMBLED ON THE END OF THIS BOOK. I WANT TO TELL YOU ABOUT JESUS WHO BROKE THE CHAINS OF ADDICTION IN MY LIFE. I WAS LOST AND HOPELESS UNTIL I MET JESUS. I HAD HEARD THAT JESUS COULD CHANGE LIVES BUT I WANTED MY SIN. MY SIN WAS FUN FOR A SEASON BUT I BECAME MORE AND MORE ISOLATED FROM PEOPLE. EVENTUALLY I WAS ARRESTED AT 17 YEARS OLD FOR BURGLARY. IN JAIL I BOWED MY KNEE TO JESUS CHIRST AND ASKED HIM INTO MY HEART. I IMMEDIETLY FELT DIFFERENT AND SLOWLY GOD BEGAN TO CHANGE ME.

IF GOD DID IT FOR ME, HE CAN SET YOU FREE. PRAY THIS AND ASK JESUS INTO YOUR HEART:

LORD JESUS, I KNOW I AM A SINNER. I ASK YOU TO CHANGE ME AND COME INTO MY HEART. I KNOW AND BELIEVE THAT YOU DIED AND ROSE FROM THE DEAD. FROM THIS DAY FORWARD I WILL LIVE FOR YOU. I

By Joshua L Neal

SURRENDER MY HEART AND MAKE YOU LORD OF MY LIFE

IN JESUS NAME AMEN

THE BIBLE SAYS THAT THE ANGELS REJOICE OVER ONE SINNER WHO GETS THEIR HEART RIGHT WITH GOD!

www.ingramcontent.com/pod-product-compliance
Lightning Source LLC
LaVergne TN
LVHW051036070526
838201LV00010B/223